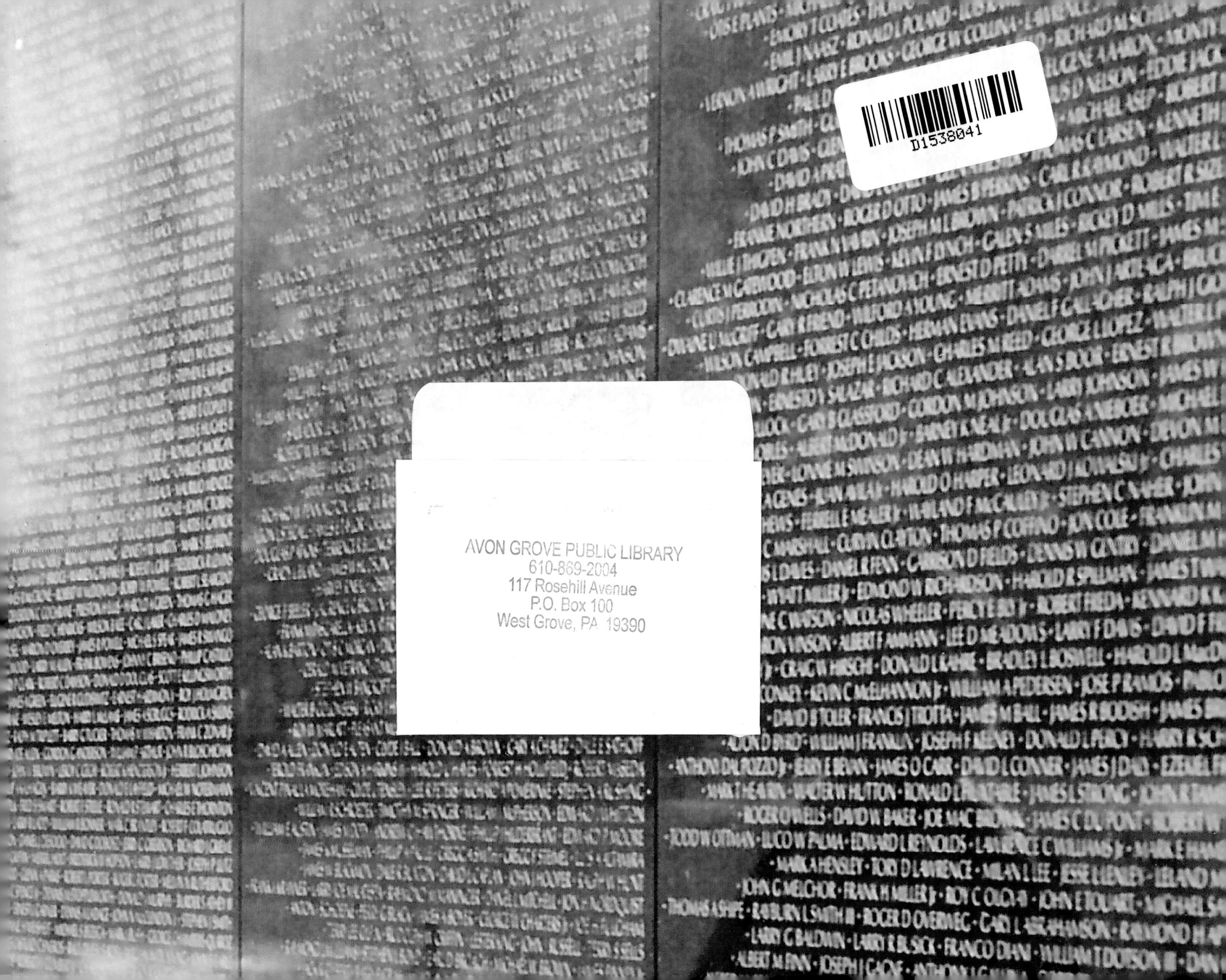

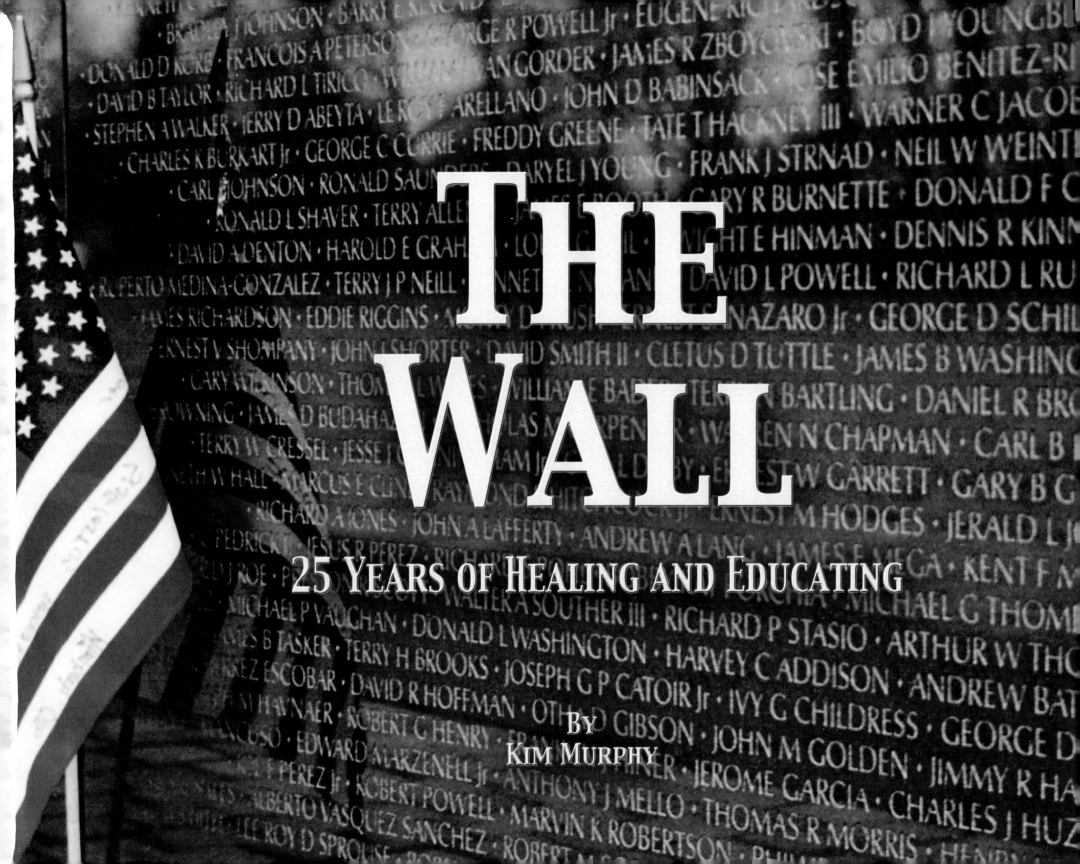

THE WALL

25 Years of Healing and Educating

By
Kim Murphy

Dedicated to all the men and women
who served and sacrificed
in the Vietnam War
and
in all wars.

Welcome home.

This Wall is our home.

It is the place that we come to extend our arms and gently draw our fingers over a name etched in granite, and for those few seconds, we feel the real presence of the people that we miss, the people that we love, the people that have sacrificed their lives.

This Wall is our home.

It is the place that we come with our eyes moist with tears and think back, sometimes to everyday occurrences that were so sweet and so good: the faces of those that we lost at birthday parties blowing out candles on top of cakes, of Christmas mornings being up to our ankles in toys and wrapping paper. It's the simple things that mean so much, the special occasions: birthday parties, graduations and family get-togethers. Also some images and scenes that aren't so easy to remember, that aren't so easy to recall, that aren't so easy to relive: hot zones and hostile fire.

This Wall is our home.

It is a place that we come to bring pictures, notes, flowers and cards and silently salute men and women from every town, from every city, from every neighborhood and from every block. Not the famous, the privileged, not the entitled. We salute those men and women who, when they put on the uniform said: "Yes, even if it costs me my life. Yes, even if it means that my days with you will be few and shortened. Yes." We can never forget that.

This Wall is our home.

It is a place where we affirm that a true sacrifice is never really made until it is accepted or received by the ones who go on. And when we touch this Wall and we see our reflection, that is the completion of the sacrifice. We are told, "Please go on, live your life well. Be people of character, honesty and dignity." The reflection back says, "Please live well. Look what I gave for you. Take this gift and complete it. Live your life; remember me."

This Wall is our home.

Mark Rumley
Brother of Robert Patrick Rumley Jr. (Panel 14E, Row 95)
Excerpt, Memorial Day Observance Ceremony Speech 2006

This is the story of The Wall.

VIETNAM VETERANS MEMORIAL FUND
1982 ~ 2007
25TH ANNIVERSARY OF THE WALL

M.T. PUBLISHING COMPANY, INC.
P.O. Box 6802
Evansville, Indiana 47719-6802
www.mtpublishing.com

The materials were compiled and produced using available information. M.T. Publishing Company, Inc., and the Vietnam Veterans Memorial Fund regret they cannot assume liability for errors or omissions.

Graphic Designer: Alena L. Kiefer

Library of Congress Control Number:
2007928647

ISBN: 978-1-932439-76-2

Printed in the
United States of America

OUT OF 2,500 BOOKS PRINTED THIS BOOK IS NUMBER

_408_.

Photos front & back cover, inside front cover and title page by Daniel Arant

Photo page 2 & 3 by Mark Segal © 1984

VVMF

4

Daniel Arant

CONTENTS

Acknowledgements 6

Introduction by Mrs. Ronald Reagan 7

Foreword by Jan C. Scruggs 8

Chapter 1: Building The Wall 9

Chapter 2: About The Wall...41

Chapter 3: The Names...53

Chapter 4: The Vietnam Veterans Memorial Fund.....................................69

Chapter 5: Volunteeers 105

Chapter 6: The Vietnam Veterans Memorial Collection 127

Chapter 7: The Impact of the Vietnam Veterans Memorial.....................143

Appendix 1: Vietnam Veterans Memorial Fund Board of Directors......181

Appendix 2: Vietnam Veterans Memorial Fund Staff 183

Appendix 3: Vietnam Veterans Memorial Volunteers 185

Appendix 4: For More Information...187

Index..205

Acknowledgements

Book Editor and Project Coordinator

Lisa Gough is the director of communications for the Vietnam Veterans Memorial Fund. She is an award-winning writer with over 20 years of experience as a magazine and book editor. She has a bachelor's degree in journalism from West Virginia University.

Writer

Kim Murphy is a freelance writer from Vienna, Va. She has 22 years of writing experience and has four books to her credit, including *The Wall That Heals*, her first project for the Memorial Fund that she co-wrote with Jan Scruggs in 1992. She has a bachelor's degree in speech communications from the University of North Carolina at Wilmington.

Photo Editor

Sara McVicker worked for the Department of Veterans Affairs for 27 years before retiring in 2006. She is a Vietnam veteran who served in the Army Nurse Corps from 1968-71, including a tour in Vietnam from 1969-70 at the 71st Evacuation Hospital in Pleiku. She is a graduate of the University of North Carolina Chapel Hill School of Nursing and Emory University.

Photo credits:

Photos in this book are credited individually. The Vietnam Veterans Memorial Fund would like to thank these photographers for donating photos for this book: Terry Adams, Linda Anderson, Amelia Arria, Jim Bannion, Tom Estrin, Bill Gray, Monica Healy, Leroy Lawson, Bill Lecky, Ed Leskin, Maya Lin, Walter Smith, Sara McVicker, Tom Morrissey, Mariah Payne, Bill Petros, Barclay Poling, Donna Prince, Dave Scavone, Jan Scruggs, Mark Segal, William Shugarts, Rajni Sood, S.J. Staniski, Holly Rotondi and the Rumley Family.

We would also like to thank the Veterans of Foreign Wars, the Non Commissioned Officers Association, the Air Force Memorial Foundation, the White House, the U.S. Senate, Smithsonian, the National Park Service and the Museum Resource Center for contributing photographs.

Very special thanks go to Dan Arant, who has been photographing The Wall and its visitors for years. Without his many photographs, this book would not have been possible.

Leroy Lawson

INTRODUCTION
BY MRS. RONALD REAGAN

It's hard to believe that it has been 25 years since the dedication of the Vietnam Veterans Memorial. In the course of our eight years in Washington, my husband and I participated in many similar events. But the day "The Wall" was dedicated stands out in my memory with special clarity.

My connection to the Vietnam War and those who served our country in that conflict had begun many years earlier. During my husband's two terms as governor of California, I visited veteran's hospitals and spent time with soldiers who had been wounded in Vietnam. I felt gratitude to them for the sacrifices they made in the service of their country and great sorrow that they were not welcomed home as the heroes they truly were. I soon became involved in the issue of prisoners of war and was deeply moved by the plight of these soldiers and their loved ones who waited for them at home. I marveled at the strength and bravery of the families who didn't know if their husbands and sons were still alive, but never lost hope. And when the POWs were released, to me it was the high point of my husband's years as governor. We held dinners in our own house to welcome these soldiers back home again. We listened to the terrible stories of their captivity, wondered at their courage and thanked them for their loyalty and patriotism.

So when the Vietnam Veterans Memorial was given to the American people during my husband's presidency, the day had personal meaning for us. We had mourned those who had lost their lives in Vietnam in the service of their country. We had empathized with those who had survived, but whose homecoming lacked the celebration and recognition they deserved. And we still grieved for those soldiers whose fate was unknown and for their families who still waited for their return. America needed a monument to help us remember and to help us heal. And most of all, we needed a monument that would inspire us to fully honor those who gave their all in the cause of freedom.

For 25 years, visitors have found a certain peace at The Wall. They leave offerings: flowers, flags, messages and items whose significance is known only to the giver. A few years after the ceremony we attended, my husband and I visited the Memorial again. And this time we left a note, our own offering to the heroes of the Vietnam War: *"Our young friends – yes, young friends, for in our hearts you will always be young, full of the love that is youth, love of life, love of joy, love of country – you fought for your country and for its safety and for the freedom of others with strength and courage. We love you for it. We honor you. And we have faith that, as He does all His sacred children, the Lord will bless you and keep you, the Lord will make His face to shine upon you and give you peace, now and forever more."*

Nancy Reagan

First Lady Nancy Reagan and President Ronald Reagan visit The Wall.

VVMF

FOREWORD

By Jan C. Scruggs

"Thank you America…for finally remembering us."

That is what I said 25 years ago when the Vietnam Veterans Memorial was dedicated on the National Mall. By that time, veterans had been struggling for at least a decade for recognition of their service to America in the Vietnam War, and the Vietnam Veterans Memorial Fund had been working since 1979 to build a tangible monument to facilitate that recognition. It all came together in November 1982, and those of us who served were overcome with joy and awe when the Memorial was unveiled.

Almost as soon as it was constructed, this 492-foot-long horizontal work of art became known as The Wall. The Wall was an instant success in Washington, D.C., attracting round-the-clock visitation from Vietnam War participants and from tourists curious to see and feel this new Memorial.

Because, indeed, touching The Wall is a key part of the whole experience. One visitor told me, "You don't go see it, you experience it. You experience it by touching The Wall, as The Wall touches you."

It did not immediately occur to me that this was a rather poignant comment.

The Wall does touch people and moves them to think about the sacrifices and casualties of the Vietnam War. Some find an even more universal statement there about those who have given their lives in all of America's military conflicts. There is tragedy inherent in military conflict. There are noble goals and what seem to be important national reasons for each war that America enters into. Yet, each must be fought by young Americans, many of whom remain forever young by giving their lives on geographically distant battlefields, ranging from Normandy Beach to Iwo Jima and beyond. Every citizen of our nation owes them all a debt of gratitude.

The Wall is one place where this debt is acknowledged.

In 1993, theologian Gustav Niebuhr wrote a piece in *The New York Times*. He opined that The Wall is akin to other revered places, such as Gettysburg, the battleship Arizona in Pearl Harbor, the Alamo and the bridge at Concord, Massachusetts, where Americans come to commune with their shared history and national identity.

In the article, he quoted respected American theologians like professor Ed Linenthal of the University of Wisconsin, who stated, "People make pilgrimages...to be transformed intellectually and spiritually at a place of power." The Wall, in a brief period of time, became transformed into a national shrine.

For Vietnam veterans, The Wall is a place where these pilgrimages and reunions take place every day.

Rolling Thunder is one example. Every Memorial Day, more than 100,000 motorcycle enthusiasts from across America meet at the Pentagon parking lot and ride to The Wall to show their support for those who are missing in action. This astounding annual display by motorcycle-riding Americans is one of many annual events by groups of veterans who feel a connection with this unique and popular Memorial.

I hope that you enjoy this book. The story of the creation of The Wall is captivating and shows that citizens can certainly have an impact when they petition the government and get involved. The story behind The Wall was, in the words of former U.S. Sen. Charles Mathias, "the work of many hands."

The Memorial has continued to help heal the wounds of our nation and has served the country well. The Wall has appeared in movies and television shows for over two decades. It has even, literally, saved lives through Project RENEW™, the ongoing humanitarian effort of the Vietnam Veterans Memorial Fund that has removed thousands of land mines in the Quang Tri Province of Vietnam.

It is astounding to realize that there are five replicas of the Vietnam Veterans Memorial that have been traveling through the United States, some for over 20 years. Most are half-scale, but one is three-quarter scale. The various replicas have even traveled internationally to England and Ireland. This speaks to the overwhelming power and popularity of The Wall.

Other memorials in Washington, D.C. and elsewhere are also relevant, as they honor our nation's important leaders and historical events. Yet few memorials anywhere have had such a legacy and ongoing impact as do these two walls of polished black granite.

Our premier project now is the Vietnam Veterans Memorial Center. It will be a place where millions of America's youths will learn poignant lessons about citizenship in a place unlike any other in the world. The Memorial Center will have synergy with The Wall and the Lincoln Memorial, both of which will be close by. It will honor not only all those who served and sacrificed in Vietnam, but also all who have fought for our freedom since we began striving as a nation over 200 years ago.

Since the year 2000, the struggle for this facility has been fraught with skirmishes against those determined to stop the project. We have prevailed because of grassroots efforts involving many hands, ranging from veterans groups and labor unions to former U.S. presidents.

In the words of Honorary Chairman Gen. Colin Powell, USA (Ret.), "It is fitting that America should have such a place to reflect on stories of courage and heroism. When it is completed, I am confident that the Memorial Center will serve as a poignant reminder that the freedoms that Americans enjoy are bought with a price."

This is the same type of reminder that the Vietnam Veterans Memorial has provided to this nation for 25 years.

These words are inscribed at the bottom of Panel 1 West.

OUR NATION HONORS THE COURAGE, SACRIFICE AND DEVOTION TO DUTY AND COUNTRY OF ITS VIETNAM VETERANS. THIS MEMORIAL WAS BUILT WITH PRIVATE CONTRIBUTIONS FROM THE AMERICAN PEOPLE.

Daniel Arant

CHAPTER 1
BUILDING THE WALL

SERVICE MEMBERS IN VIETNAM

- Over 3.4 million personnel served in the Southeast Asia Theater.
- 2.59 million men and women served in Vietnam.
- One out of every 10 Americans who served was a casualty.
- More than 58,000 died and 304,000 were wounded.
- 75,000 Vietnam veterans were severely disabled, suffering amputations or crippling wounds.

Statistics courtesy of VFW Magazine

Courtesy of Jan Scruggs

BUILDING THE WALL

On Jan. 21, 1970, Jan Scruggs was having his morning cup of coffee, but he was far from the kitchen table of his boyhood home. He was in Vietnam, serving in the 199th Light Infantry Brigade.

In the nine months since he'd been in-country, Scruggs had already seen a lot of action, having been wounded in a battle fighting North Vietnamese Army troops in Xuan Loc. He had spent three months recovering in a hospital, before being sent back to fight with rocket-propelled grenade fragments permanently embedded in his body.

On that January day, "There was a big explosion. I ran over to see a truck on fire and a dozen of my friends dying," recalled Scruggs. The 12 had been unloading an ammunition truck when the explosion occurred. Scruggs would never forget the blood, the screams, the carnage. He would never forget those friends.

In fact, he would spend a lifetime trying to honor their memory.

Scruggs was raised in a rural Maryland town, nestled amid the horse farms that stretch between Baltimore and Washington, D.C. His mother was a waitress; his father a milkman. "We're all the result of our upbringing. My background was relatively modest," Scruggs said. "But I was always impressed with the example my parents set."

Courtesy of Jan Scruggs

When the 18-year-old Scruggs volunteered to enlist in the Army in 1968, debate surrounding Vietnam was escalating. Its length and the growing number of casualties were fueling tensions. Within months after Scruggs recovered from his wounds and returned to his unit, the American public was learning the details of the massacre at My Lai. By the time he returned home, three months after the explosion, the country was even further divided.

"That was a bad time. The anti-war movement was at its zenith. My age group was very opposed to the war," recalled Scruggs. "Not many people had much sympathy for those who had fought there." He remembered being on a first date once, when the girl began to tell Scruggs about her outrage at discovering that a former boyfriend had served in Vietnam. "She was absolutely appalled that she had gone out with someone who had been there, someone who had 'done these awful things,'" he recalled. Scruggs never told her that he too had served. It didn't seem worth mentioning. He knew he wasn't going to see her again.

Over the next few years, as the war came to a close and more and more troops returned home, the media began to focus on the fact that many veterans were failing to adjust to life back in the States. They painted a picture of veterans as drug-addicted, bitter discontents. The truth was, while veterans were becoming increasingly outraged by the way they had been—and were still being—treated, they weren't any more likely to be addicted to drugs than their non-combat counterparts.

And, who could blame them for being bitter? The vast majority of Vietnam veterans, just like Scruggs, were kids when they left home to go to war. Many had barely been out of high school when they answered their country's call to service. Yet when they returned home, there was no national show of gratitude. If they were lucky, they were greeted with silence and stares. The unlucky were shouted at and called vicious names. Veterans frequently found themselves denying their time in Vietnam, never mentioning their service to new friends and acquaintances for fear of the reactions it might elicit.

By June 1977, Scruggs had been married for three years to Becky, a young woman he met the year after he returned home. He was attending graduate school at American University in Washington, D.C. and had embarked on a research study exploring the psychosocial consequences of Vietnam military duties. He was becoming intimately aware of the impact of society's treatment on veterans and those around them.

Courtesy of Jan Scruggs

His results showed that returning veterans were finding it hard to trust in people; feeling alienated from the nation's leaders; and experiencing low self-esteem. He also found that those veterans whose units experienced high casualty rates were experiencing higher divorce rates and a greater frequency of combat-related dreams. Using his findings, he testified at the Senate hearing on the Veteran's Health Care Amendments Act of 1977, with the hope that he could help veterans gain access to the services and support they needed.

He wanted to find a way to help them heal.

(Above) Jan Scruggs recovers at the 6th Convalescent Center, Cam Ranh Bay, 1969.

(Left) Pictured are the members of Company D, 4/12, 199th Light Infantry Brigade, 1969.

(Previous page) Jan Scruggs on his last day in Vietnam: April 2, 1970.

Daniel Arant

The Idea of a Memorial

Hollywood was also focusing its lens on veterans and memorializing Vietnam on film. Movies like "Heroes" and "Coming Home" humanized the issues plaguing veterans. That same year, Congress discussed creating a Vietnam Veterans Week to honor the veterans who had returned home. Their plight was slowly gaining attention.

Then, "The Deer Hunter" hit theaters and presented some of the most powerful war scenes ever depicted. It told the story of three factory workers from a small town in Pennsylvania who are drafted and sent to Vietnam. The movie explored the meaning and the effects of war on the three friends, their families and a tight-knit community.

When Scruggs went to see "The Deer Hunter" in early 1979, it wasn't the graphic war scenes that haunted him. It was the reminder that the men who died in Vietnam all had faces and names, as well as friends and families who loved them dearly. He could still picture the faces of his 12 buddies, but the passing years were making it harder and harder to remember their names.

That bothered him. It seemed unconscionable that he or anyone else should be allowed to forget. For weeks, he obsessed about the idea of building a memorial. Perhaps a memorial, inscribed with all of their names, similar to those built in Europe after WWI to honor fallen troops, could help change that.

"It just resonated," he explained. "If all of the names could be in one place, these names would have great power. A power to heal. It would have power for individual veterans, but collectively, they would have even greater power to show the enormity of the sacrifices that were made."

His research had given credence to post-traumatic stress and had shone a light on the challenges faced by a significant number of military veterans. When the idea for a memorial sprang forth, it seemed a natural extension of his work and his growing desire to find a way to help veterans.

Scruggs took two weeks off from his job at the Department of Labor to develop the idea further. He studied the writings of Carl Jung, a student of Sigmund Freud who wrote about collective psychological states. The basic theory was that, just as veterans needed psychological healing, so too did the nation. He planned to rally people as diverse as former anti-war presidential candidate George McGovern and Gen. William Westmoreland, who commanded U.S. forces in Vietnam, to support the project. Money was a problem, but Scruggs sold a piece of land he inherited for $2,800—not much, but it was enough to hire a lawyer to incorporate the project and hold a press conference.

"The idea of the Memorial was multifaceted," he explained. "It would help provide a psychologically cathartic experience for veterans who would be able to see the names of their friends who were casualties of the war. The Memorial's mere existence would be societal recognition that their sacrifices were honorable rather than dishonorable. Veterans needed this catharsis, and so did the nation. The nation needed something symbolic to help heal the divisive wounds."

(Previous page) Many Purple Hearts have been left at The Wall.

(Right) Jan Scruggs announces plans at the National Press Club in Washington, D.C. to build a national memorial dedicated to all those who served in the Vietnam War, Memorial Day 1979.

Building a Coalition

When Scruggs set his mind to something, he was relentless in his focus and persistence. His wife Becky recalled first learning of his idea. "He just came out one day and announced that this was what he was going to do. I was a little taken aback. It shocked me. But it wasn't like he was asking me my opinion," she laughed. It was more of a declaration: he was going to build a memorial.

As congressional efforts to pull together a Vietnam Veterans Week continued, Scruggs decided to attend one of the meetings to announce his plans. With a roomful of veterans, he figured the idea would receive resounding support. Instead, the majority grumbled about his naiveté and cautioned him that Congress would never support such an effort. They wanted more benefits and government support, they shouted.

But one veteran, a former Air Force intelligence offer and an attorney named Bob Doubek, was struck by the idea.

"When I was attending law school, there was no talk at all about Vietnam among the young single professional set of Washington," remembered Doubek. "There was no talk of anyone's experience there. You didn't know if another man had served in Vietnam or not. Of course, I had met some of the best people in my life in the military in Vietnam. It seemed unfair and inappropriate that there should be no mention of the war. I really felt what was needed was recognition."

Doubek approached Scruggs after the meeting and suggested that he form a nonprofit organization to formalize his efforts to build a memorial. On April 27, 1979, Doubek incorporated the fledgling group, the Vietnam Veterans Memorial Fund, for a $500 fee. He was genuinely interested in the effort, so Scruggs asked him to join the Memorial Fund board of directors, and Doubek agreed.

VVMF

One of their initial efforts involved holding a press conference on Memorial Day to announce their plans to raise $1 million to build a memorial. While media coverage of the announcement was slim, it prompted a handful of supportive letters and a few small donations. Still, it was far from the floodgate response Scruggs had boldly predicted during the press conference.

By July, the Memorial Fund had collected only $144.50, a fact that was reported by Roger Mudd on the "CBS Evening News" and lampooned on late-night television. While vacationing at the beach in South Carolina, Jack Wheeler came across a brief newspaper article on the Memorial Fund, its mission and its minimal progress to date. Wheeler, a graduate of West Point, Yale Law School and the Harvard Business School, had served in Vietnam. He had also spearheaded the effort to build a Southeast Asia Memorial at West Point. He understood the types of challenges that building a national memorial would pose.

Wheeler reached out to Scruggs. Although very different from one another, it was clear from their first meeting that the two shared a common vision to honor those who had served in Vietnam and a similar, single-minded "can do" attitude.

The Memorial Fund began recruiting others to help, ending up with a group of professional men, all Vietnam or Vietnam-era veterans, comprised of George "Sandy" Mayo, Art Mosley, Dick Radez, John Morrison, Paul Haaga, Bill Marr and certified public accountant Bob Frank, who agreed to become the Memorial Fund's treasurer.

During that time, Doubek attended a dinner party with three other couples. Amazingly, all four men had served in Vietnam. Over the course of the night, they talked endlessly about the war, sharing stories and memories. It was the first time that they could remember talking openly about their experiences to anyone who actually cared to listen. And it felt good.

One of the men at the party was John Woods. Woods was a U.S. Army captain and a helicopter pilot who was shot down on Oct. 26, 1967. He spent three years recovering from his injuries, retired from the military on disability and went on to become a structural engineer. In Woods, Doubek saw the much-needed expertise that it would take to guide the building of a memorial.

Woods remembered Doubek's call. "I thought the idea was a good one, but I had no clue how you would go about getting the job done," he said.

The greatest challenge the Memorial Fund faced, said Doubek, was "to put together a functioning organization with people who didn't know one another, people who were very young and didn't have a lot of experience. We had to constantly find the most effective next step to take and be sure not to get waylaid by tangents."

For Woods, the growing coalition was a prime example of "it's not what you know, it's who you know." These people, though a small group, were able to reach out to their networks and their extensive contacts to recruit the type of expertise and support required for such a mammoth initiative. Their military experience meant they had contacts far and wide, at all levels of all professions, within government and the private sector. It seemed every time they contacted someone, they were greeted with enthusiasm for the idea. Everyone wanted to join the effort. And if they themselves didn't know how to help, they knew someone who did.

Their initial timeline was aggressive, with an ultimate goal of dedicating the Memorial on Veterans Day 1982, just a little more than 36 months away. The list of tasks to achieve such a goal seemed endless. They needed to secure a plot of land, raise funds and public awareness, design the Memorial, coordinate construction and plan the dedication festivities. Most importantly, they needed to navigate the channels of government and do it swiftly.

Never in the history of the United States had a national memorial been conceived, approved, built and dedicated in that short amount of time. Even memorials that enjoyed overwhelming support languished for years in one phase or another of the approval process. The Franklin Delano Roosevelt Memorial Commission was established in 1955; yet it was not until May 1997 that the memorial was completed, dedicated and opened to the public.

If the challenges seemed insurmountable, no one uttered their fears or trepidation. And none of them discussed their own personal feelings or political views regarding the war. All of them realized how critical it was that a memorial be apolitical. They set their sights in support of the clear, simple vision Scruggs outlined: to honor the warrior and not the war.

A U.S. Army trumpeter plays taps during a ceremony at The Wall.

GARNERING CONGRESSIONAL SUPPORT

Scruggs decided one of his first calls to garner support would be to the senator of his home state of Maryland, Charles "Mac" Mathias. A Navy veteran of World War II, Mathias had been opposed to the war in Vietnam.

Mathias was a seasoned politician, having served more than 25 years in public office. Known as a man of conscience in the Senate, he was a Republican who represented a Democratic state. "He believed that the government was an instrument to help people help themselves," explained Monica Healy, a long-time Mathias staffer. "People liked him personally. He had a great way of going right to the heart of a matter. He had good peripheral vision and could see all sides of an issue." Mathias was well read, loved foreign affairs and had a strong sense of history.

After Scruggs left a message for the senator, Mathias called to set up a meeting so he could learn more. "It was really hard to get a meeting with the senator," Healy said. "A lot of his constituents wanted to meet with him, but he only had so much time. The fact that Jan got on his schedule was a big deal. It meant that Mathias thought it was really important."

"I had my ear to the ground," Mathias recalled. "I heard there was a group of serious veterans, not just people getting together to have a beer in the evening, but a group that was serious about getting together to address the problems of the veterans."

Scruggs, Doubek and Wheeler met with Mathias to outline their plans. As they did, they stressed that all funds for the Memorial would be raised from private donations. No government funds would be necessary. What they did need, however, was an acceptable location for the Memorial and enough support to push the idea through various governmental committees and agencies.

"Initially the [senator's] staff was split," Healy recalled, "on whether Mathias should take the lead and support the efforts to build the Memorial. The senior staffers were against it. It was the senator's gut feeling that we needed to do this."

Mathias had grown increasingly concerned about how veterans had been treated on their return. He had also spent ample time visiting the Antietam battlefield and monuments. Because he possessed great knowledge of history, he understood the extensive healing process required after war. A memorial made perfect sense to him. It would be a way to honor the veterans and to help them — and the country — to heal.

"This was serious business," Mathias said. "You had to live through that period to really understand it...But the veterans had real problems. They needed support, friendship and help. And that message got through to me."

Mathias also knew the country was ready, Healy recalled. Timing is everything, and enough time had passed. Intellectually and emotionally, America could embrace the idea.

In many ways, Mathias was cautious, only occasionally being out front on issues. So, when he stepped up not only to support the Memorial, but also to lead the effort, it spoke volumes to those around him.

One of Mathias' early key suggestions was to bypass the traditional site selection route and have Congress pass legislation to award a specific plot of land to the veterans for use as a memorial site. He identified the ideal spot: a stretch of parkland known as Constitution Gardens, located on the National Mall adjacent to the Lincoln Memorial.

"It was important to have a spot that was clear and uncluttered," Mathias said. "This was before the Mall was crowded...We got an old Esso gas station map of Washington, D.C., brought it into the waiting room at the Senate Office Building and spread it out on the table. There was a representative

After the bill authorizing a memorial to Vietnam veterans passed in the Senate, those who worked for its passage gathered for a photo. Jan Scruggs is pictured in the center giving the "thumbs up." Others are, from left: Murray McCann; Lt. Cmdr. Jerry Bever, USN; Bill Marr; unidentified man; Ron Gibbs; Sen. Charles "Mac" Mathias (R-Md.); Sen. Robert Dole (R-Kan.); Jan Scruggs; Tom Carhart; Sen. Dale Bumpers (D-Ark.); Bob Doubek; Arthur Mosley; unidentified man; Jack Wheeler; Bill Jayne; and Bruce Spiher.

Senate Photographer

from the National Park Service there, and that was when we made the decision."

"He [Mathias] looked at the map, put his finger on the spot and said 'This is what we want,'" Healy recalled. Mathias wanted the Memorial where the anti-war demonstrations had been. In addition, she said, "He cared that wherever it was, it worked aesthetically."

As a "big picture" thinker, Mathias put a tremendous amount of faith in his staffers. "If you learned his style, you worked really well with him," said Healy. Among other duties, Healy was the staffer who handled memorials and worked as the liaison with the U.S. Department of the Interior. Mathias appointed her to manage the details and to work with Scruggs, Doubek and Wheeler.

At the time, and for several months that followed, Healy was the only woman working on behalf of the Memorial. "I was the unlikely candidate," she said. "I demonstrated against the war at the University of Maryland. I didn't have anyone in my family who went to Vietnam. I didn't have any friends who went, and I didn't have that deep feeling of what the impact of war had been."

But Mathias knew that she was relentless, persistent and highly goal oriented. "Maybe he had a sense of how difficult it was going to be," she chuckled.

Healy, Scruggs, Doubek and Wheeler worked together on a daily basis. "The three of them had different strengths," Healy explained. "Jan was a great spokesperson. Bob was the detail person, who was a good writer. Jack was the visionary, the creative, big-picture guy. They really worked well together and were the driving force. Jack, Jan and Bob were on the Hill every day lobbying. It was such a great cause, and they were bound and determined to make it happen."

As they forged a partnership with Mathias and his staff, the Memorial Fund also set out to establish other key relationships. Scruggs took a bold step in contacting Virginia Sen. John Warner by letter. Scruggs' "can do" spirit appealed to Warner, who had served as Secretary of the Navy during the latter part of Vietnam and was himself a veteran of World War II and the Korean War.

From the outset, having one senator who had been a proponent of the war and one who had opposed the war seemed a critical strategy to the theme of reconciliation. In the instance of Mathias and Warner, both senators were Republicans, but they made a great, balanced team. Warner was more conservative, able to appeal to staunch Republicans, while Mathias could appeal to Democrats and the more liberal members of his party.

Because Warner was from Virginia and Mathias from Maryland, the two had worked together on many regional issues. They were comfortable with each other, respected one another and knew each other's strengths. "We had been friends for a long time," Mathias said. "He was an excellent partner and fundraiser." Mathias knew the legislative process. Warner, at the time married to Elizabeth Taylor, had strong connections to both Hollywood and the corporate world.

On Nov. 8, 1979, the Memorial Fund held a press conference in which Mathias, Warner and several others announced plans to introduce legislation that would grant two acres of land near the Lincoln Memorial for the Vietnam Veterans Memorial.

Monica Healy

Courtesy of Monica Healy

A MOTHER'S STORY

Bill Petros

Emogene Cupp,
American Gold Star Mother

Scruggs and Doubek scouted around town, looking for shared office space that might be suitable for the Memorial Fund. They called on Emogene Cupp, then the national president of the American Gold Star Mothers. "Jan and Bob came to our headquarters to see if we had any room to help them get started," Cupp remembered. "We didn't have any space, but I liked their idea and told them I would volunteer to help with all that I could."

The Gold Star Mothers is a group of mothers whose sons or daughters have died serving their country. Their motto is: "Honor the dead by serving the living." Volunteering to assist the Memorial Fund was an ideal opportunity for Cupp to do just that.

Cupp had experienced firsthand the pains caused by Vietnam. Her only son Robert had been drafted into the Army. He was killed on his 21st birthday, June 6, 1968, after he stepped on a land mine. Compounding the pain was the fact that society's ill treatment toward veterans extended to their families. "It was very hurtful," Cupp recalled. "They treated the moms the same as they treated the vets. They weren't nice. At that time they just ignored you and wished you would go away. Or, people would tell me, 'Well why did you let him go?' Of course, what choice do you have?"

A few months after Robert's death, the local Alexandria, Va. chapter of Gold Star Mothers contacted Cupp, who proceeded to become involved in the organization, rising to serve as its head by 1978.

Once Scruggs and Doubek met Cupp, they knew she could be instrumental in helping them communicate the all-important personal, emotional side of the healing story. Cupp began to accompany the two to many of their meetings on Capitol Hill as they drummed up support.

FUNDING THE EFFORT

Just before Christmas 1979, the Memorial Fund embarked on an aggressive fundraising effort led by Warner, who hosted a fundraising breakfast in his Georgetown home that was not easily forgotten by those who attended. Warner made an impassioned plea for funding to his guests, members of the defense industry. As he spoke, all eyes turned toward the staircase. His then-wife, actress Elizabeth Taylor, walked down the stairs in a regal fashion, wearing a bathrobe, perfect makeup and beautiful shoes that curled up at the toes. "I'm sure I looked like a deer in the headlights, I was so nervous," Scruggs recalled. "I think I even spilled my coffee." But, her presence made a difference. "I heard that those present agreed to double their contributions after Taylor completed her remarks," Scruggs said.

Around the same time, the Memorial Fund also launched its first large-scale direct mail campaign, hoping to reach out to the public and enable them to be a part of building the memorial. To structure these efforts, they formed the National Sponsoring Committee, which included then-First Lady Rosalynn Carter, former President Gerald Ford, Bob Hope, Nancy Reagan, Gen. William C. Westmoreland, USA, James Webb and Adm. James J. Stockdale, USN.

The first fundraising letter was signed by Bob Hope. It echoed the theme that regardless of how anyone felt about the war itself, everyone cared about honoring the men and women who had served and those who had ultimately lost their lives.

By early 1980, contributions started to arrive. Some of the larger early donations came from corporations such as Gruman Aircraft and from such individuals as H. Ross Perot.

Direct mail was proving to be a highly effective fundraising tool. Heartfelt notes written by individuals across the country arrived, accompanied by checks and dollar bills. Letters came from moms, dads, grandparents, sons and daughters. They came from veterans and from the neighbors, teachers, coaches and friends of veterans. The public wanted to have a hand in helping to build the Memorial and in honoring the warrior, not the war.

As work continued, the Memorial Fund realized it needed to increase its fundraising goals; $1 million would not be enough money to build a memorial. The goal was increased to $2.5 million, and staff members stepped up their efforts, often working 12-hour days, six days a week.

Scruggs began hiring people. He was impressed with Marine Corps Col. Don Schaet, an effective manager and hard-core Marine who saw

combat in Vietnam. After some persuading, he finally agreed to leave the Marines and become the Memorial Fund's vice president.

As the Memorial Fund focused on fundraising, Sens. Mathias and Warner continued to rally support and ferry the legislation. Although there was some opposition to the Memorial from the anti-war movement, Mathias and Warner continually stressed that their objective was to provide the country with a symbol for reconciliation.

"There were so many people helping to get the legislation [passed]," remembered Healy. "The more people you got to co-sponsor, the more people wanted to join. When we started, we didn't know if the legislation was going to be controversial or not. At some point, you have to jump in."

On April 30, 1980, the Senate approved legislation authorizing the Memorial, followed by approval in the House on May 20, 1980. Both were adopted unanimously. On July 1, a ceremony was held in the Rose Garden where President Jimmy Carter signed legislation providing two acres for the Vietnam Veterans Memorial on the National Mall.

(Right) The core group of individuals who worked to ensure the passage of the bill creating a Vietnam Veterans Memorial includes, from left: Sen. Charles Mathias (D-Md.); Jack Wheeler; Monica Healy; Jan Scruggs; and Bob Doubek.

(Far right) President Jimmy Carter signed the law authorizing the Vietnam Veterans Memorial to be built on the National Mall on July 1, 1980.

Courtesy of Monica Healy

White House

BUILDING THE WALL 17

The Vietnam Veterans Memorial is seen from above before a ceremony.

The Memorial's Design

With the land approved, the Memorial Fund scrambled to address the issues of what the Memorial would look like and who would design it. A few preliminary concepts were embraced. As Scruggs had always envisioned, the Memorial would feature all of the names of those who had died. Wheeler suggested that it should be a landscaped solution: a peaceful, park-like setting which could exist harmoniously with the Washington Monument and the Lincoln Memorial.

They were also keenly aware that the legislation made the Memorial's design subject to the approval of the Commission of Fine Arts (CFA), the National Capital Planning Commission (NCPC) and the Secretary of the Interior.

It was decided that the Memorial Fund would hold a design competition. Just as the Memorial Fund hoped to help the American people be a part of building the Memorial through their contributions and support, they could also enable all Americans to have an opportunity to participate in its design.

They hired architect Paul Spreiregen to serve as the contest advisor. Spreiregen, a graduate of the MIT School of Architecture and Planning, was a Fulbright Scholar who had served as the director of urban design programs at the American Institute of Architects (AIA) from 1962-66 and as the first director of architecture programs at the National Endowment for the Arts from 1966-70. An author, teacher and lecturer, Spreiregen had conducted extensive research on the subject of design competitions.

At the time, well-managed open design competitions were common in Europe, but not in the United States. Most, like the Lincoln Memorial, were competitions between select designers. Only a few, such as the St. Louis Gateway Arch, part of the Jefferson National Expansion Memorial, had been the result of a well-managed, open competition.

Of his hiring, Spreiregen wrote, "I saw this as a needed opportunity to honor the service and lives of the soldiers we had lost and do so by running a model competition. I had no illusions about the likelihood of achieving anything. At the time, the American public wanted to forget Vietnam."

For three solid months, Spreiregen, and the Memorial Fund planned the competition. "We had to build credibility among the design community, but also build credibility with the veterans," said Woods. "The design competition also needed to be able to attract design competitors."

There were six phases to the design competition spanning a little more than one year: planning and preparation; launching the competition; the design phase; the design evaluation and selection; the press conference and public presentation; and the public agency approval and project mobilization.

"The first phase encompassed the detail planning and preparations for holding the competition," said Spreiregen. "Holding a competition is like launching a rocket. Everything has to be thought out and in place before the launch button is pressed."

The Design Criteria

Traditionally, war memorials were erected to commemorate great victories. They usually featured a building, monument or statue. After World War I, most memorials in small villages and towns across Europe would feature a plaque with the names of locals who had died. A few, like the Thiepval Memorial honoring the 72,000 who died battling on the River Somme in Northern France, were far grander and larger scaled.

But this was not a "war memorial." Instead, the intention of the Vietnam Veterans Memorial was to honor those who had served and those who had died for their country.

"A memorial is a permanent dedication in behalf of commemoration—remembering together. It is an act of appreciative recollection through which the past informs the present," explained Spreiregen.

The Memorial Fund drafted guidelines for the competition, outlining that each design must: be reflective and contemplative; harmonious with the site, as well as with the Washington Monument and the Lincoln Memorial; and make no political statement about war. "The hope is that the creation of the Memorial will begin a healing process," Doubek wrote.

Healing meant many things to many people. Could a memorial accomplish such an enormous and daunting task? Could it heal the chasm within society, promote closure, show gratitude to those who served, comfort those in grief and remind future generations of the toll wrought by war? Moreover, could it accomplish all of that while listing the approximately 58,000 names in an artistic, meaningful way?

Selecting the Jury

Selecting a design which would meet the criteria demanded a jury that could grasp the significance of the Memorial's purpose and understand the unique needs of Vietnam veterans, their families and a country divided. For weeks, heated discussions took place around the topic of who should be part of the design jury. Many felt it should be composed primarily of veterans; others felt it should be made up only of professionals; some thought a mix of the two would be best.

Although Spreiregen did not share his opinion with the Memorial Fund, he felt strongly that the jury should be made up of professionals. "It would be very difficult to choose which type of Vietnam Vet would be right. One who had been there at the beginning or at the end? One who was wounded? An officer or an enlisted man? A 'grunt' or a flier? A medic or a company commander? A POW? Who could be sufficiently representative?

"I regard the role of jurors as absolutely vital to a successful competition...jurors must be people of great professional achievement in their own right," he continued. "They must be able to deliberate articulately...be highly experienced in working with clients and with public agencies and groups. They must know the characteristics of the area where the project is to be located, in this case Washington, D.C. They must represent the various fields of design from whose ranks one hopes competitors will be attracted to the competition."

Board member Art Mosley researched the topic. Based on what he learned, he was adamant about having an all-professional jury. Ultimately, the Memorial Fund board followed Mosley's advice.

Spreiregen recommended eight people, or "senior gray eminencies," seven of whom were to be selected. There were two professionals representing the fields of architecture and landscape architects; three representing the world of sculpture; and one who was a journalist with extensive experience writing about architecture and landscape design. It was expected that only two of the sculptors would be chosen to sit on the panel.

Before being selected, it was a requirement that each read *Fields of Fire* and *A Rumor of War*, the current literature on Vietnam. In addition, Spreiregen suggested that all eight have the opportunity to meet with the Memorial Fund board, so that an impartial decision could be reached. The Memorial Fund met the prospective jurors and scrutinized their credentials. "I doubt that any of the VVMF staff had ever met, let alone talked with, designers of the stature of those jurors," recalled Spreiregen. "They found that they

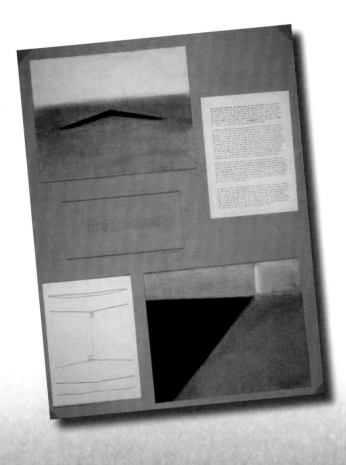

were very real people who did many of the same things they did. They were real guys. The VVMF group liked them all and approved of them with trust and enthusiasm," even selecting all three sculptors.

The jury included: architects Pietro Belluschi and Harry Weese; landscape architects Hideo Sasaki and Garrett Eckbo; sculptors Costantino Nivola, Richard Hunt and James Rosati; and Grady Clay, journalist and editor of *Landscape Architecture*. Four of the eight jurors were themselves veterans of previous wars. "Many had worked together, some in Washington. They were also the most collegial people, who would deliberate intensely but never argue or posture," Spreiregen remembered.

ANNOUNCING THE COMPETITION

With the jury selected, the next task was to announce and promote the competition. In the fall of 1980, the Memorial Fund announced that it would hold a national design competition open to any U.S. citizen who was 18 years or older. By year's end, it had received 2,573 registrations from individuals and teams. From the registration forms, it was apparent that architects, artists and designers — of all ages and all levels of experience — were planning to participate. They came from all parts of the country and represented every state. By the March 31, 1981 deadline, a total of 1,421 designs had been submitted.

With such an overwhelming response to the competition, logistics became an issue. End-to-end, the total number of submissions would have stretched 1-1/3 linear miles. The judging criteria stated explicitly that each submission needed to be hung at eye level for review by the jury. But how and where could all of the submissions be displayed?

Vietnam veteran Joseph Zengerle, then an assistant secretary of the Air Force, volunteered the use of an empty hangar at Andrews Air Force Base. The added component of military security made the location even more attractive, since it could ensure that no anti-war or anti-military groups would try to vandalize or destroy the submissions in protest.

In accordance with the strict competition guidelines, anonymity of all designs was carefully observed. Each contestant sealed his or her name in an envelope and taped it to the back of the submission. The designs were received and processed in a large mail-order warehouse east of Washington. They were unwrapped, number coded, photographed for the record and prepared for display nearby.

LET THE JUDGING BEGIN

Memorial Fund board members struggled to understand how a suitable design was going to result from the competition. There were so many expectations and complex emotions attached to the Memorial. "We were all sitting in our offices one day—Bob Frank, Sandy Mayo, me, Jan and Jack," recalled Woods. "And someone said, 'I just don't believe how this will work.' I said, 'My guess is there will be a designer who comes in with a simple, elegant design.'" Woods understood the design community. He knew it was possible for someone to take the guidance and input the Memorial Fund had provided and create a winning design. He encouraged the group to continue to have faith in the process.

Another concept that was hard to grasp was all that the jurors would consider during their deliberations. "There are maybe 50 different 'considerations' in exploring a design possibility," Spreiregen explained. "They encompass all that

Maya Lin's submission to the design contest is show at the top. Above is a close-up of her watercolor rendering of the design.

Both photos: VVMF

a design must do: how the design will exist in its setting to how people will experience it; how it will be built to how it can be maintained and how it will age; how the various conditions of light affect how it will be seen to what is called its 'style' or system of visual expression — and so very much more. In Washington, a public design also has to be able to weather an intensive if not grueling design review process. That's part of it, too. You have to be able to get approval to build your design."

Only a professional, Spreiregen felt, was capable of looking at a simple depiction and quickly judging if it had merit, if it was buildable and appropriate, if it could be built within a reasonable budget and if it fit the site.

The jury evaluation took place over five days, from April 27 through May 1, 1981. They started by touring the site together, although each had already previously visited the location. Then they returned to Hangar #3 at Andrews Air Force Base to view each of the 1,421 designs individually. "I had calculated that it was possible to see all of them in a minimum of 3-1/2 hours. The eldest juror, Pietro Belluschi, took a full day," said Sprieregen. "By the end of the first afternoon, one of the jurors, Harry Weese, returned to our impromptu conference lounge and told me, 'Paul, there are two designs out there that could do it.'

"On the second day, the jury examined the designs together, walking the many aisles and stopping at each of the 232 designs that had been flagged by one or more of the jurors, pausing to discuss each design that had been noted. The first cut was further reduced to 90 by midday Wednesday. By Thursday morning, it was down to 39. That afternoon, the winning design was selected," said Spreiregen.

"It was the most thoughtful and thorough discussion of design that I have ever heard, and I have heard many," he recalled. As an example of their thoroughness, one juror made a sketch showing how easily The Wall could be constructed. Another noticed that someone might accidentally wander across the grass above The Wall, and accidentally fall over the edge to the ground below. The jury proposed that a low "trip wall" be added on the higher ground, several feet away from the edge, to protect visitors. The trip wall was added to the final design.

With the winning design in hand, Spreiregen had less than 24 hours to craft an explanation of the decision, and the design, that would be suitable for presentation to the Memorial Fund. Throughout the judging process, Clay had taken meticulous notes of the jury's discussions. Together with Spreiregen, he composed a report based on these thoughtful comments.

MAYA LIN'S DESIGN

Design entry number 1026, which was unanimously selected by the jury, belonged to Maya Ying Lin, a 21-year-old Chinese-American architecture student who was attending Yale University.

For her senior project, she decided to work with a group of students studying funereal architecture. The previous year, she had traveled abroad in Denmark and had been struck by the way areas within European cities had multiple uses. Norbrow, in Copenhagen, she explained in an interview for the Academy of Achievement, was "this enormous park, probably half the size of Central Park, that was also a cemetery...[In Europe] your cemeteries are habitable...they're parks." When she returned to Yale, her studies expanded to include the nature of the monument, what it is and what it should be.

As the group of students began working on their assignments, one of them stumbled on a bulletin announcing the competition for the Vietnam Veterans Memorial. They decided to use that as the foundation for their projects, although Lin had no notion of entering the design in the competition.

One day, they traveled together to the site of the planned memorial. There, sitting on the grass as people played Frisbee nearby, the idea came to her. "I knew it when I saw the site. I wanted to cut it open and open up the earth and polish the earth's edges. Then came the embellishment of the names."

Lin wanted to create a park within a park, a quiet, protected place for people to reflect. In an interview with *The Washington Post* years later, she said, "It was a beautiful park. I didn't want to destroy a living park. [As an architect/designer] you use the landscape. You don't fight it. You absorb the landscape...When I looked at the site I just knew I wanted something horizontal that took you in, that made you feel safe within the park, yet at the same time reminding you of the dead."

SUBMITTING HER DESIGN

Within weeks of returning to Yale, after her trip to Constitution Gardens, Lin completed her design as part of her senior project. It consisted of two polished, reflective black granite walls, or arms, in a chevron or expansive "V" shape. Each wall grew, sinking low into the ground, with the earth behind it. One arm pointed directly to the Washington Monument to the east, while the other pointed west to the Lincoln Memorial.

"What the Vietnam Veterans Memorial had to be was about honesty, about dealing up front with individual loss," Lin later

Walter Smith

Maya Lin

Once Maya Lin's idea was selected, architects constructed a model of how it would look on the National Mall.

explained to the Academy of Achievement. "The most important thing I thought was the acknowledgement of loss. We have to face it. If we can't face death, then we'll never overcome it. So, as opposed to pretending it never happened, you have to look it straight in the eye. Then you can turn around and walk back into the light."

In creating the design, "I deliberately did not read anything about the Vietnam War," Lin recalled. "I really felt the politics of the war eclipsed what happened to the veterans. The politics were irrelevant to what this memorial was...there were people on that Wall who were for it. There were people on that Wall who were against it. I wanted to offend neither of them. That was a huge goal. So I did not want to know anything about the politics behind the war."

Critical to her design was the order of the names. "I wanted the names in chronological order because, to honor the living as well as the dead, it had to be a sequence in time," Lin told Robert Campbell in an article for the AIA journal.

Her professor, Andrus "Andy" Burr, reviewed a clay model of her design. He told her, "You have to make the angle mean something." With Burr's feedback, she revised the design to have the names begin and end at the apex of the walls.

"At the intersection of these walls, on the right side, at the wall's top, is carved the date of the first death. It is followed by the names of those who have died in the war, in chronological order," Lin wrote in the narrative which accompanied the design. "These names continue on this wall, appearing to recede into the earth at the wall's end. The names resume on the left wall, as the wall emerges from the earth, continuing back to the origin, where the date of the last death is carved, at the bottom of this wall. Thus the war's beginning and end meet; the war is 'complete,' coming full circle."

As part of the project review process, Lin presented her design to a room full of visiting architects who critiqued her work. Some felt that she should change the black granite walls to white marble, but she stood firm on her approach.

ANNOUNCING THE WINNER

With no fanfare, Lin mailed her submission to the competition on the last day it could be postmarked. Her rendering, mixed media on paper mounted on board, had an ethereal quality but lacked the usual details inherent in a professional design.

On Friday, May 1, 1981, Spreiregen and Clay presented the jury's decision to the Memorial Fund. Of the evaluation comments captured by Clay that were used in their presentation, Spreiregen wrote, "They are a treasure of design insight

and included many prescient thoughts as to how the Memorial would likely be experienced."

Some of the juror comments included:
"Many people will not comprehend this design until they experience it."
"It will be a better memorial if it's not entirely understood at first."
"Confused times need simple forms."

According to the description of the design concept:
"The jury chose a design which will stimulate thought rather than contain it."

In part, the jury's official statement read:
"Of all the proposals submitted, this most clearly meets the spirit and formal requirements of the program. It is contemplative and reflective. It is superbly harmonious with its site and yet frees the visitors from the noise and traffic of the surrounding city. Its open nature will encourage access in all occasions, at all hours, without barriers. Its siting and materials are simple and forthright.
"This memorial with its wall of names, becomes a place of quiet reflection and a tribute to those who served their nation in difficult times. All who come here can find it a place of healing. This will be a quiet memorial, one that achieves an excellent relationship with both the Lincoln Memorial or Washington Monument and relates the visitor to them. It is uniquely horizontal, entering the earth rather than piercing the sky.
"This is very much a memorial of our own times, one that could not have been achieved in another time and place."

Spreiregen and Clay spent 25 minutes presenting the design to the Memorial Fund. "When we concluded, there was a brief moment of silence," Spreiregen recalled. "Jan Scruggs got up and said to all, with heartfelt enthusiasm, 'I like it.' Immediately the whole group jumped to their feet and started hugging each other in joy. They really got it. They really understood what the memorial design was all about, why we recommended it."

"A lot of excitement had built up, a lot of work led up to the design competition. When we heard that the jury had selected one, it was very exciting to get in the car and go over there to see it," Scruggs recalled of that day.

"It was a design that was difficult to understand until the jury explained it to you," he added. "That became the problem,

Jan Scruggs, Maya Lin and Bob Doubek unveil the model of the Vietnam Veterans Memorial.

really. That's why others took issue with it, and I can see their point. The average person does not have the skill set to look at something in two-dimensional art and fast-forward to what it will look like as a more than 400-foot structure. But it was apparent to me that it would be a very handsome stone with qualities that other stones would not have, for example, that you could see your own reflection in the names."

When Scruggs learned that the designer was Maya Ying Lin, a name of obvious Asian descent, he was relieved. "It showed that the design process was fair, that it had worked, that the background of the person was irrelevant" to the selection of a winner, he said.

Woods remembered that day as well, "We were dumbfounded that there was a unanimous decision by the jury. To get artists to agree is unreal.

"They showed us the top three designs," he recalled. "I don't remember the third one, but I remember that the second place winner was a traditional war memorial that glorified war. Then they showed us these pastels that Maya had produced. But it was her description of what she was portraying that had so much meaning...this simple, elegant solution.

"Maya's thought was that The Wall was only one element of the Memorial," Woods continued. "The whole Memorial was the entire park-like setting. Each person [who visits] is part of the Memorial. My reflection becomes part of the Memorial. I can think back as I look at the walls. She designed it to be contemplative."

With the design selected, attentions turned to announcing the winner. It was felt that Lin's renderings were not sufficient for public debut at a press conference. As a few representatives from the Memorial Fund headed to Yale to notify Lin and ask that she return with them to Washington for the press conference, Spreiregen worked with juror Harry Weese's office to create two models of the display. One model depicted the Memorial and its placement within the context of the Mall; the other showed the Memorial design itself. Once the models were complete, they photographed them and created a presentation slide show, as well as press kit materials. "We realized that the story was to be as much about Lin as it was the design," Spreiregen said. "The press conference would have to be love at first sight or the project was dead in the water."

On May 6, 1981, a press conference was held in a crowded board room at the headquarters of the American Institute of Architects. It was a tremendous success, generating numerous positive national news stories and television reports.

Within days, the annual Armed Forces weekend was held at Andrews Air Force Base. On Saturday, May 9, the doors to Hangar #3 were opened so that the public could view all of the design submissions. A crowd filled the hangar the entire time.

Maya Lin, accompanied by members of the building team, displays the model of the Memorial on the actual site. From left: Architect of record Kent Cooper; John Marquart and Bill Choquette of the Gilbane Building Company; Maya Lin, designer; Bob Doubek; and Bill Lecky, Cooper-Lecky Partnership.

Early on in the effort to get the Memorial built, there were traces of controversy. Some felt that the money to build a memorial could be better spent delivering the many services veterans needed. Others questioned the intent of the Memorial. Throughout, Scruggs embraced the discourse. Only by no longer ignoring the war and its veterans could the country truly begin to heal. Besides, the controversy helped draw attention to the Memorial, something that was critical to fundraising.

Months before the design competition commenced, the Memorial Fund realized that it once again needed to increase its budget figures, to as much as $7 million in order to fund a memorial fully. The pressure was on for board members, staff and volunteers, particularly for Sandie Fauriol, the woman hired to lead the fundraising efforts. At the same time, grassroots efforts to raise money were beginning to sprout across the country. Organizations such as The American Legion, the Veterans of Foreign Wars (VFW) and the American Gold Star Mothers threw their support behind the efforts. Many gave large donations. Children in schools took up collections, and individuals across America continued to give.

When the Memorial Fund announced the selection of Lin's design, the initial public reaction was overwhelmingly positive. "We were finally getting the attention from the media that we had sought from the beginning," Doubek wrote. "Though the unconventional design provoked some negative comment, a consensus favoring its elegant simplicity emerged on the part of the architectural critics, the staffs of the approval bodies and veterans organizations."

But several weeks after the announcement, a handful of people began to protest the design. A few of the most vocal opponents, James Webb and H. Ross Perot, had previously been strong supporters of a memorial. They complained about the walls being black. They did not like the idea that it was below ground level. They felt it was a slap in the face to those who had served because it did not contain traditional symbols honoring service, courage and sacrifice. Some opponents simply did not like the fact that Lin was a young student, a woman and a Chinese-American; how in the world could she possibly know how to honor the service of the Vietnam veteran?

"The minimalist design accomplishes little," said Scott Brewer, a Vietnam vet, in a July statement delivered before CFA. "I find it to be abstract, anonymous, inconspicuous and meaningless, and is so unfulfilling as a lasting memorial that no memorial would be a better alternative."

Then, in October 1980, veteran and writer Tom Carhart, also a former supporter, testified before CFA against the design, saying that "One needs no artistic education to see this design for what it is, a black trench that scars the Mall. Black walls, the universal color of shame and sorrow and degradation." He followed that appearance with an article in *The New York Times*. The media pounced on the controversy and helped his phrase, the "black gash of shame and sorrow," sprout wings.

From the first moment he saw Lin's design during the jury's presentation, Scruggs said, "I was convinced that we had some public relations challenges ahead and some controversy, although I didn't really predict it would spin out of control. The opposition was a small group of influential people who were very good at politics. But they were not alone in their views. They represented many other people who didn't understand the design."

Even Scruggs' wife Becky was baffled by it. "When the jury picked the design, Jan showed it to me before the press conference," she recalled. "My reaction was it looked like a bat. I didn't really like it at all, but I didn't say that, because this renowned jury had picked it, so there must have been something to it that I didn't understand or know."

While the controversy made headlines, it also made fundraising easier. The Veterans of Foreign Wars (VFW) began promoting the idea of the Memorial and soliciting donations from their local posts through direct mail. At that time, there were between 9,000 to 10,000 local VFW posts. According to Doubek, by December, VFW presented a check for $180,000. (Over the course of the entire effort, VFW contributed as much as $300,000 through a combination of donations from individual members and the organization.) The American Legion was also busy raising funds and was quickly approaching its $1 million goal.

While Memorial Fund staffers were relieved that donations were pouring in, they struggled with how to react to the escalating controversy. There was no arguing that both sides wanted a memorial. Their goals were the same. At issue was what type of memorial would be most fitting. The greatest risk, according to Doubek, was that if they lost the battle to build the Lin design, they would lose the memorial entirely. "The strong consensus and momentum could never be regained, as each new design proposal would be second-guessed for decades," he stated.

"We talked about it [the controversy] constantly," Becky Scruggs recalled. "At times, I tried to help Jan keep things in perspective. Other times, I got emotional at what was happening. It was very much a rollercoaster ride. Although, I actually found it to be exciting, the ups and downs of it, occasionally it was overwhelming...but the good times outweighed the bad."

Lin also struggled with how to handle the controversy. Her relationships with many of those involved were precarious and strained. As discussions began on the construction of the Memorial, she wanted an ally in the process, someone she could trust to fight for her design. She approached a contact at the Yale School of Architecture and asked for a recommendation of a firm in Washington that could join the project. He suggested the Cooper-Lecky partnership. The Memorial Fund interviewed several firms, eventually selecting Cooper-Lecky and hiring Lin as the project's design consultant.

Bill Lecky recalled the first time he and his partner Kent Cooper saw Lin's design. "We thought it was a very powerful, elegant statement," he said. "There was page of writing included on her presentation boards that was a beautifully written description of the experience of going to the Memorial. I'm sure that writing ultimately got her the award and overcame the quality of the drawings."

Unfortunately, such eloquent descriptions had done nothing to sway the opposition's opinion. It appeared the opposition might have the power to halt the project in its tracks, despite the fact that the design had been approved by the Commission of Fine Arts and the National Capital Planning Commission. "We had obtained preliminary approval in just over two months since the design had been procured," said Spreiregen. "Compared to any other recent memorial effort, this was something of a record."

"What I didn't realize at the time," Healy recalled, "was how one small group is all it takes" to shut down an entire initiative. "The opponents were skillful and smart in knowing who to call and how to stop it."

"We thought it would be received by the public with great admiration and understanding," said Mathias. "We didn't know it was going to be quite as controversial as it was. We had a tough time with some of the original donors to the Fund, who wanted to have [the Memorial reflect] their personal ideas of what they thought it should look like."

By early 1982, the Memorial Fund asked Warner to bring together both sides for a closed-door session to hammer out the issues. According to Healy, it was strategic to have Warner lead the meeting. He, better than Mathias, would be more effective at appealing to the veterans who had broken ranks.

VVMF

A Feb. 22, 1982 article by Hugh Sidey in *TIME* magazine described the session: "A few days ago, 40 supporters and critics of the memorial gathered to try to break the impasse that threatened the memorial because of such features as the black color of the stone and its position below ground level. After listening for a while, Brigadier General George Price, retired, stood in quiet rage and said, 'I am sick and tired of calling black a color of shame.' General Price, who lived with and advised the 1st Vietnamese Infantry Division, is black."

In fact, Gen. Price's speech that day ended the controversy over the black granite and the use of the term "black gash of shame" forever.

To Heal a Nation, the book written by Jan Scruggs and Joel Swerdlow that tells the story of the building of The Wall, gives a vivid sketch of the scene:

"'I have heard your arguments,'" General George Price, one of America's highest ranking black officers said. 'I remind all of you of Martin Luther King, who fought for justice for all Americans. Black is not a color of shame. I am tired of hearing it called such by you. Color meant nothing on the battlefields of Korea and Vietnam. We are all equal in combat. Color should mean nothing now.'"

Sidey's *TIME* magazine piece continued: "At the end of five hours and much shouting, General Mike Davison, retired, who led the Cambodian incursion in 1970, proposed a compromise: add the figure of a soldier in front of the long granite walls that will bear the 57,709 names of those who died or are missing and the tribute to all who served. The battle was suddenly over."

Gen. Price had been working with the Memorial Fund since its earlier days. "These young men finally got to me," he said of that moment when he stood up to put a stop to the color debate. "Black was not a color of shame. We had proven that over and over again...and I also resented the fact that anyone would discuss Maya Lin's heritage in terms of her design."

The Memorial Fund's main goal was to ensure that nothing threatened to "disfigure or destroy the imposing image of the design," Price explained.

As the heated talks progressed, he and Gen. Davison decided together that it would be better for Davison to present the idea to add a sculpture as a compromise. "We knew it may not have the same effect if I made the proposal rather than him," Price added.

The Memorial Fund agreed to the statue compromise, as well as to adding a flag and an inscription on the Memorial, but they did not want to wait until a statue was designed before breaking ground. Waiting meant they would never reach their Nov. 11 dedication deadline.

Both sides worried that CFA and NCPC, who had ultimate approval of the flag and statue, might not support the addition of such elements. Breaking ground while the compromise was negotiated would allow them to proceed. Yet some wondered whether that meant the Memorial would get built while the statue and flag languished eternally in the approval process. Then, Secretary of the Interior James Watt dealt the Memorial Fund a crushing blow. He threatened not to issue a construction permit unless both CFA and NCPC approved the compromise.

Over several tense weeks, more debate followed, until CFA and NCPC gave their approval for a statue and flag, pending suitable placement of those elements. Watt followed on March 11, 1982 by granting permission for the construction permits.

"No matter how many obstacles there are, if the cause is right, you have to keep going," Healy said of the many lessons learned from that time.

The design's merits overcame the critics, said Mathias. "I'm glad we hung on and prevailed. It was a remarkable exercise in dedication on the part of the veterans," he added. "They were not without differences of opinion, but they were all resolved in favor of the Memorial...I've been involved with many organizations, but very few have shown the level of personal commitment that was shown."

With permit in hand, Scruggs met a construction crew at the site. "Make this place look like an airstrike was called in," he instructed. "Rip it apart." His reasoning was that a complete mess would make it tough to stop construction.

An official groundbreaking ceremony was held on March 26, 1982. Sen. Warner's assistant, Andy Wahlquist, had an idea. Get 100 veterans—two from each state—and give them shovels to break ground. Gen. Price, along with Sens. Warner and Mathias and future Sen. Chuck Hagel, gave moving addresses before the command was given, and 100 shovels entered the ground with enthusiastic veterans enjoying the moment.

But, much work was still ahead. They now had only eight months to build The Wall.

(Previous page) Ground is broken for the Vietnam Veterans Memorial on March 26, 1982.

(This page, right) A Vietnam veteran is overcome with emotion after the groundbreaking ceremony. Other veterans offer comfort.

S. J. Staniski

(This page) Many believe the location of the Three Servicemen statue gives the impression that they are emerging from a grove of trees and happen upon The Wall.
(Opposite page) A visitor stops to read the sign designating the site where the Three Servicemen statue will be placed prior to its addition in 1984.

Leroy Lawson © Frederick E. Hart/VVMF, 1984

28 BUILDING THE WALL

ADDING THE STATUE

In early April 1982, as construction crews tore up turf on the Mall, the Memorial Fund created an independent panel to ensure the successful selection of a statue and eliminate any threat of controversy during its design. The panel included two opponents and two supporters of Lin's design. The four would have to arrive at a consensus in order to please both sides. The panelists were James Webb and Milt Copulos, who opposed Lin's design, and Art Mosley and Bill Jayne, who supported it.

Jayne had worked as a volunteer for the Memorial Fund early on, focused on public relations. That work led to a job opportunity within the government. In order to avoid any conflicts of interest, he scaled back his time with the Memorial Fund but maintained his contact with Scruggs and the group. Jayne was also a combat veteran during the Tet Offensive and had been slightly wounded.

"Like most people, I was very impressed by the Memorial's design," Jayne recalled, "[the] way it conveyed all of the names without seeming to bore people. It didn't become a 'yellow pages,' it was more than a directory. I personally was stymied by how to convey all of those names. I was also impressed with the idea of the polished black granite being reflective, [so that] people would see themselves in it. Plus, it meant a lot the way it connected the Vietnam experience with American history, the way it pointed to the Washington Monument and the Lincoln Memorial."

Because of his work on behalf of and his belief in the Memorial, Jayne felt honored to be asked to join the sculpture panel. "I wanted to do everything possible to smooth out the controversy, which was very disheartening and worrisome to everyone."

The panel contacted Frederick Hart, a well-known and respected sculptor whose team had placed third in the open design competition. While conducting research prior to entering the design competition, Hart had spent an enormous amount of time studying Vietnam and interviewing veterans. During that time, he cultivated relationships with Scruggs, Doubek, Wheeler and Webb.

"We weren't sure how we were going to forge ahead," Jayne said. "We talked a lot with Hart and ended up meeting several times at his studio. It was neutral ground and was easily accessible. We talked about what the sculpture should accomplish."

The panel's hope was that Hart's creation would be "representational, true to life, and in effect, put a face on the names," said Jayne.

Hart's early models involved a single soldier, which appeared too lonely. After several meetings and discussions, Hart delivered a model featuring three figures. Immediately, the group knew it was the ideal concept. "My original thought was: 'Our work is done. This is going to do it,'" said Jayne.

From there, they worked with Hart to add the appropriate level of detail that would resonate with veterans. Webb had kept a pair of old jungle boots that Hart used as a reference. Webb also obtained some authentic combat gear for Hart to study. "On the figures, there are different kinds of flak jackets," explained Jayne. "One has on a Marine jacket, with its plates more obvious, while the other wears an Army-styled jacket, and one isn't wearing a jacket." There are other details, as well, that are true to service in Vietnam.

On Sept. 20, a model of the sculpture was unveiled to the public. The final piece, known as "The Three Servicemen," is a slightly larger-than-life depiction of three infantrymen cast in bronze. The men—one white, one black and one Hispanic—are all in uniform, two carrying weapons.

Hart said this in describing the sculpture: "They are young. The contrast between the innocence of their youth and the weapons of war underscores the poignancy of their sacrifice. There is about them the physical contact and sense of unity that bespeaks the bonds of love and sacrifice that is the nature of men at war...Their strength and their vulnerability are both evident."

Lin strongly opposed the addition of both the statue and the flag. Supporters of the statue and the flag wanted to have the flag at the vertex and the statue

in the angle, Doubek recalled, in effect making The Wall a pedestal for the flagpole and a backdrop for the sculpture. Rather than viewing them as additions, Lin regarded them as changes which violated the integrity of her work and altered the entire nature of the Memorial. The Memorial Fund was caught in the crossfire between political critics and various factions of the arts community.

After enduring months of controversy and the frenzied construction process, Lin grew weary and resigned from the project. "She asked us to resign as well," Lecky recalled. But Cooper-Lecky chose not to resign. "Our position was that if we left," Lecky explained, "then no one would remain who could fight the good fight."

On Oct. 12, 1982, just weeks before the Memorial's dedication ceremony was to take place, CFA recommended that the flag be grouped with the statue in order to enhance the entrance to the site.

To find just the right location for the statue and the flag, a team from Cooper-Lecky went to the Memorial grounds. "We kept backing away from the apex until we felt we had a location that was suitable," remembered Lecky. It was a location where you got the impression that the figures were emerging from a grove of trees and happening upon The Wall.

Once they determined the location for the statue, the Cooper-Lecky team reworked the walkway system, so that the flag could be placed at an intersection in order to create an entranceway. Today, the 12-foot-by-8-foot flag flies from a 60-foot pole, 24 hours a day, seven days a week, in honor of the men and women who served in Vietnam. The flagstaff, paid for by donations from The American Legion, features an inscription and the seals of the five branches of military service at its base: Air Force, Army, Coast Guard, Marine Corps and Navy.

The completed statue was unveiled on Nov. 8, 1984. "With 20/20 hindsight, the statue now seems like a good addition to the site," Doubek conceded. "A lot of people seem to really find it to be an affirmation, the literal depiction of their youth and courage."

Although the Memorial Fund held a National Salute to Vietnam Veterans in 1982 that included the dedication of The Wall, the Vietnam Veterans Memorial was not officially turned over to the government until the statue and flagpole were in place in 1984. In a Veterans Day ceremony at The Wall that year, President Ronald Reagan and First Lady Nancy Reagan accepted the Vietnam Veterans Memorial from the Memorial Fund on behalf of the American people.

Sara McVicker

Sculptor Frederick Hart included many authentic details on the The Three Servicemen statue.

Daniel Arant © Frederick E. Hart/VVMF, 1984

President and Mrs. Reagan wave to the crowd, Veterans Day 1988.

VVMF

President Reagan accepts the Vietnam Veterans Memorial on behalf of the nation on Veterans Day 1984. Behind him, from left: Jack Wheeler; First Lady Nancy Reagan; Jan Scruggs; Secretary of the Interior William P. Clark; Jane Clark; Secretary of Defense Caspar Weinberger.

White House

Remarks by President Ronald Reagan at the Dedication Ceremony
For the Vietnam Veterans Memorial
November 11, 1984

Ladies and gentleman, honored guests, my remarks today will be brief, because so much as been said over the years and said so well about the loyalty and the valor of those who served us in Vietnam. It's occurred to me that only one very important thing has been left unsaid, and I will try to speak of it today.

It's almost 10 years now since U.S. military involvement in Vietnam came to a close. Two years ago, our government dedicated the Memorial bearing the names of those who died or are still missing. Every day, the families and friends of those brave men and women come to The Wall and search out a name and touch it.

The Memorial reflects as a mirror reflects, so that when you find the name you're searching for, you find it in your own reflection. And as you touch it, from certain angles, you're touching, too, the reflection of the Washington Monument or the chair in which great Abe Lincoln sits.

Those who fought in Vietnam are part of us, part of our history. They reflected the best in us. No number of wreaths, no amount of music and memorializing will ever do them justice, but it is good for us that we honor them and their sacrifice. And it's good that we do it in the reflected glow of the enduring symbols of our Republic.

The fighting men depicted in the statue we dedicate today, the three young American servicemen, are individual only in terms of their battle dress; all are as one, with eyes fixed upon the Memorial bearing the names of their brothers in arms. On their youthful faces, faces too young to have experienced war, we see expressions of loneliness and profound love and a fierce determination never to forget.

The men of Vietnam answered the call of their country. Some of them died in the arms of many of you here today, asking you to look after a newly born child or care for a loved one. They died uncomplaining. The tears staining their mud-caked faces were not for self-pity, but for the sorrow they knew the news of their death would cause their families and friends.

As you knelt alongside his litter and held him one last time, you heart his silent message—he asked you not to forget.

Today, we pay homage, not only to those who gave their lives, but to their comrades present today and all across the country. You didn't forget. You kept the faith. You walked from the litter, wiped away your tears and returned to the battle. You fought on, sustained by one another and deaf to the voices of those who didn't comprehend. You performed with a steadfastness and valor that veterans of other wars salute, and you are forever in the ranks of that special number of Americans in every generation that the Nation records as true patriots.

Also among the service men and women honored here today is a unique group of Americans whose fate is still unknown to our nation and to their families. Nearly 2,500 of the names on this Memorial are still missing in Southeast Asia, and some may still be serving. Their names are distinguished by a cross rather than the diamond; thus, this Memorial is a symbol of both past and current sacrifice.

The war in Vietnam threatened to tear our society apart, and the political and philosophical disagreements that animated each side continue to some extent.

It's been said that these memorials reflect a hunger for healing. Well, I do not know if perfect healing ever occurs, but I know that sometimes when a bone is broken, if it's knit together well, it will in the end be stronger than if it had not been broken. I believe that in the decade since Vietnam, the healing has begun, and I hope that before my days as Commander in Chief are over, the process will be completed.

There were great moral and philosophical disagreements about the rightness of the war, and we cannot forget them, because there is no wisdom to be gained in forgetting. But we can forgive each other and ourselves for those things that we now recognize may have been wrong, and I think it's time we did.

There's been much rethinking by those who did not serve and those who did. There's been much rethinking by those who held strong views on the war and by those who did not know which view was right. There's been rethinking on all sides, and this is good. And it's time we moved on in unity and with resolve—with the resolve to always stand for freedom, as those who fought did, and to always try to protect and preserve the peace.

And we must in unity work to account for those still missing and aid those returned who still suffer from the pain and memory of Vietnam. We must, as a society, take guidance from the fighting men memorialized by this statue. The three servicemen are watchful, ready and challenged, but they are also standing forever together.

And let me say to the Vietnam veterans gathered here today: When you returned home, you brought solace to the loved ones of those who fell, but little solace was given to you. Some of your countrymen were unable to distinguish between our native distaste for war and the stainless patriotism of those who suffered its scars. But there's been a rethinking there, too. And now we can say to you, and say as a nation: Thank you for your courage. Thank you for being patient with your countrymen. Thank you. Thank you for continuing to stand with us together.

The men and women of Vietnam fought for freedom in a place where liberty was in danger. They put their lives in danger to help a people in a land far away from their own. Many sacrificed their lives in the name of duty, honor and country. All were patriots who lit the world with their fidelity and courage.

They were both our children and our heroes. We will never, ever forget them. We will never forget their devotion and their sacrifice. They stand before us, marching into time and into shared memory, forever. May God bless their souls.

And now I shall sign the document by which this Memorial has been gratefully received by our government.

And now it belongs to all of us, just as those men who have come back belong to us all. Thank you.

President Reagan spoke at 4:30 p.m. at the Vietnam Veterans Memorial on the National Mall. The Three Servicemen Statue, by sculptor Frederick Hart, was dedicated at the ceremony. Following his remarks, the president signed documents transferring the Vietnam Veterans Memorial to the federal government.

The Salute

As soon as groundbreaking for The Wall began in March 1982, so did the planning for its dedication ceremonies. For months, word traveled that a massive National Salute to Vietnam Veterans would take place that Veterans Day. The American Legion, VFW, Disabled American Veterans (DAV), AMVETS and Paralyzed Veterans of America (PVA) made sure their members knew that veterans were going to be honored and welcomed that week on the National Mall. More than 150,000 veterans, families, loved ones and friends made plans to attend.

The series of events began on Wednesday, November 10, 1982 and culminated with the dedication of The Wall on Saturday, November 13.

The Salute opened with a vigil Wednesday morning at the National Cathedral, where all of the nearly 58,000 names on The Wall were read by volunteers around the clock, day and night, through midnight Friday. Every 15 minutes, there was a pause for prayer.

On Saturday, a grand parade took place where veterans marched joyously out of sync, some hand-in-hand or with their arms draped around one another, holding banners, flags and signs. Many pushed friends in wheelchairs. The following week, Kurt Anderson recapped the festivities for *TIME* magazine: "Saturday's three-hour parade down Constitution Avenue, led by [Gen. William] Westmoreland, was the vets' own show. The 15,000 in uniforms and civvies, walked among floats, bands and baton twirlers. The flag-waving crowds even cheered."

Over the four days there were also workshops, parties, events and reunions. "It was like a Woodstock atmosphere in Washington for those who had served in Vietnam," recalled Scruggs "After three-and-a-half years of nonstop effort and work, with all that you have to do to accomplish what we did, it was beautiful. It was surreal."

"The whole week was extremely emotional," Becky Scruggs remembered. "It was a whirlwind of events, and the press coverage was unbelievable. I remember *The Washington Post* had pages and pages of stories in the 'A' section." Vietnam veterans were, at long last, receiving the recognition they deserved.

Woods remembered, "I was like the kid at FAO Schwartz. I was dumbfounded that we had succeeded at doing this. The controversy overshadowed the mission and what we were doing," until the Salute brought it all together.

After the dedication, Scruggs and Wheeler walked together along the upper side of the Memorial ground, near Constitution Avenue. Although thousands of people were there, "It was so very quiet," Wheeler recalled. "I just kept thinking to myself how quiet it was, and yet there was an immense feeling of community. It was becoming apparent that we had been able to be instruments to something far greater than anything we had ever imagined."

Doubek also remembered something odd that happened that week. His story would be one of many "Wall Magic" stories to spring up over the years—stories in which unexplained coincidences happened at or because of The Wall. In the final days before the Salute, construction and landscaping crews were trying to keep the crowds off of the newly laid sod using fences around the Mall. Doubek was down at the site, wrapping up for the night. A young man approached and asked if he could go down to The Wall. Doubek asked him to return another time. The young man said he was from California and would be leaving soon, so he wouldn't be able to return.

Doubek agreed to walk the man down to The Wall. "As we were walking, I was telling him how the [panels] are like pages in a book. He was getting emotional. I had the directory with me. So we looked up the location of this name, then he thanked me and left."

The morning after the dedication, Doubek and his wife were watching Charles Kuralt on "CBS Sunday Morning." Kuralt traditionally ended the show with a snippet of film, and that day, they were showing footage of the Memorial. Gradually the camera moved in closer, Doubek recalled, "until you were seeing one wall...then 10 panels...then one panel...then a few rows of names...then the camera stopped to focus on a single name...and it was the same name that the guy had asked me to see." He sat stunned for a moment, then thought to himself, "Maybe that guy was an angel telling me I've done OK."

Candlelight Vigil
of the
National Salute to Vietnam Veterans

National Cathedral
Washington, D.C.
November 10-12, 1982

VIETNAM VETERANS MEMORIAL FUND

**We Remember
We Honor**

Sponsored by the
Vietnam Veterans Memorial Fund, Inc.

Program courtesy of Sara McVicker

(Previous page) An aerial view taken from the west shows the vastness of The Wall.

(This page, right) All of the names on The Wall were read during the candlelight vigil.

South Vietnamese immigrants came to the parade to thank U.S. veterans for their service.

Sara McVicker

VVMF

A contingent from Ohio marches in the parade.

Veterans from the Standing Rock Sioux Nation participated in the National Salute to Vietnam Veterans.

VVMF

Veterans gather in front of The Wall before the dedication.
Sod is being laid on the area to the right.

Moments after the Memorial dedication, three of the men who worked so hard for its creation embrace: (from left) Sen. John Warner, Brig. Gen. George Price and Jack Wheeler.

State flags lined The Wall for the dedication ceremony

Thousands gathered for the dedication on November 13, 1982.

*The crowds were eager to get close
at the dedication of the Memorial.*

THE IN MEMORY PLAQUE

Years after the war had ended, it became clear that the toll it had taken on those who had served had not ended. Many began to suffer premature deaths related to their service. Some contracted serious illnesses brought on by exposure to Agent Orange. Others endured the consequences of post-traumatic stress disorder.

On Nov. 10, 2004, a plaque was dedicated at the northeast corner of the Three Servicemen Statue plaza, with a ceremony sponsored by the Vietnam Veterans of America. The design team that created the plaque was headed up by James "J.C." Cummings, who had worked with Maya Lin in bringing about architectural drawings for her design of The Wall. The plaque is a carved piece of black granite measuring 24 inches by 36 inches. The inscription reads "In memory of the men and women who served in the Vietnam War and later died as a result of their service. We honor and remember their sacrifice."

Since 1999, the Vietnam Veterans Memorial Fund has held an *In Memory* Day ceremony on the third Monday in April to honor all those who died as a result of the war. This yearly ceremony recognizes new honorees and all whose names are on the *In Memory* Honor Roll.

(Above) After the 2007 In Memory Day ceremony, family members place the tributes at The Wall.

(Left) The In Memory plaque honors those who died as a result of their service in the Vietnam War, but who do not meet the Department of Defense criteria to be listed on The Wall.

IN MEMORY
OF THE MEN AND WOMEN
WHO SERVED IN THE VIETNAM WAR
AND LATER DIED AS A RESULT
OF THEIR SERVICE

WE HONOR AND REMEMBER
THEIR SACRIFICE

THE VIETNAM WOMEN'S MEMORIAL

Photo by VVMF © 1993, VVMF; Glenna Goodacre, Sculptor

While the vast majority of names on The Wall belong to men, there are eight women, all nurses, whose names appear on its panels. Of the 265,000 women who served during Vietnam, nearly 10,000 military women served in-country during the conflict. Barred from combat, these women served in health care, communications, intelligence and administrative positions. Civilian women served as foreign correspondents for news agencies, worked for organizations such as the American Red Cross and the USO, or served in other government agencies, such as USAID or at the embassy.

In late 1983, Diane Carlson Evans, a nurse who served in the Army in Vietnam, conceived of the idea to add a statue to the Vietnam Veterans Memorial to honor the women who served. She incorporated the Vietnam Women's Memorial Project (VWMP) in 1984. In 2002, the group changed its name to the Vietnam Women's Memorial Foundation (VWMF).

According to VWMF, the memorial was established not only to honor those women who served, but also for the families who lost loved ones in the war, so they would know about the women who provided comfort, care and a human touch for those who were suffering and dying.

Ultimately, the Commission of Fine Arts approved a bronze sculpture created by Glenna Goodacre for the Vietnam Women's Memorial. The 2,000 pound, 6-foot 8-inch sculpture portrays three women, one of whom is caring for a wounded male soldier. It was dedicated on November 11, 1993.

(Above) The Vietnam Women's Memorial pays tribute to the thousands of women who served.

(Right) Diane Evans spearheaded the Vietnam Women's Memorial project.

(Far right) The dedication of the Vietnam Women's Memorial, on November 11, 1993, also drew crowds.

Tom Estrin

National Park Service

1959

WALL MAGIC

THE BOX
BY
RON EDGINGTON

It was late May 1996. Bill Harter and I were on duty as Wall volunteers. It was mid-morning, and visitor flow was increasing. I looked up and saw a group of about 12 high school students approaching. Two were carrying a box. They were silent and looked so serious. I looked at Bill, and he said, "This should be interesting."

Little did we know how interesting!

We learned that this was a senior's elective class on the Vietnam War from a high school in New Jersey. They were accompanied by their teacher, a knowledgeable young lady intent on providing first-hand experience in one of life's difficult lessons. Her students had read about visitor reactions at The Wall and the phenomenon of family, friends, war buddies and schoolchildren leaving very personal items—items that held a deep significance—there.

She had asked students to choose an item that held special meaning in their lives, one that could not be replaced, and to put it into the box. This, she reasoned, would illustrate their personal "loss."

The group stopped near Panel 6W and put the box down. Silently, they formed a semi-circle. Their faces showed stress.

Some looked ready to cry; all looked nervous. By now, other visitors were stopping to watch. One by one, the students would reach into the box, retrieve their thing and tell the others its meaning in their life: a little league trophy; a varsity letter; a state track medal.

One last student reached in and pulled out a photo of a "grunt" wearing a flak jacket and helmet and leaning against a bunker of sandbags. "This is my dad, and it is the only picture I have of him in Vietnam," she said. She spoke a few more tearful words, then returned the photo to the box.

By now, the crowd was large and blocking the flow of visitors. But that did not seem too important to us. We were as caught up in the emotion as those students were. As the crowd began to disperse, it was evident by the tissues in view that those kids had not only learned a lesson, they had taught one also. Bill and I knew that we had been a part of "Wall Magic."

I have been a volunteer for over a decade. For me, there is "Wall Magic" every day I am there:

When you have looked into the tear-filled eyes of a family member on his or her first visit…

When you are hugged by a Gold Star Mother…

When you are asked to do a rubbing and are told to "save room on the paper for my other son's name"…

When a 10-year-old tugs on your shirt and looks directly at you and says, "Thank you for fighting"…

When you watch 50 or so middle school students from Hawaii place fresh-cut exotic flowers at EACH panel…

When the widow of a Medal of Honor recipient asks you to help her find her husband's name…

When you have stood alone at the apex at midnight and cried…

…then you will have a better idea of just what Wall Magic is.

Ron Edgington is a Vietnam veteran and a volunteer at the Vietnam Veterans Memorial. He lives in Lincoln University, Pa.

National Park Service

Smithsonian

VVMF

ABOUT THE WALL

Maya Lin's vision was to have the Vietnam Veterans Memorial appear as a rift emerging from and receding into the earth. The Memorial was built almost exactly as she conceived it. It is two highly polished, black granite walls in a wide chevron shape. Each wall begins at ground level and grows gradually in height as it sinks low into the earth, until both meet at the vertex.

At the highest part, referred to as the apex, the walls are 10.1 feet tall. They meet at an angle of 125.12 degrees. Each wall is composed of 74 separate granite panels, 70 of which are numbered and inscribed. Each panel is 40 inches wide. Combined, the panels stretch 246 feet 8 inches on each side and are supported by 140 concrete pilings driven 35 feet into bedrock. The Wall's total length is 493 feet, 4 inches.

The wall that points to the Washington Monument is referred to as the East Wall, while the West Wall points to the Lincoln Memorial. Each panel is numbered from 1 to 70 at its base, with West Panel 1 and East Panel 1 meeting at the vertex, leading out to East or West Panel 70.

In 1982, when The Wall was dedicated, there were 57,939 names inscribed. Names have been added to The Wall almost every year since it was dedicated. *(For more information on how a name is added, see Chapter 3.)* As of Memorial Day 2007, it contained 58,256 names. The tallest panels have 137 lines of names, while the shortest have just one. An average of five names are on each line, with spaces left throughout the Memorial for name additions.

BUILDING THE MEMORIAL

Not long after Lin's design was chosen, the Memorial Fund began to consider the all-important details of building The Wall.

Vietnam veteran John Woods remembered scrutinizing the design from a structural engineering point of view. He knew it was feasible to build; it seemed rather straightforward. "It was going to be a reinforced concrete retaining wall, set on pilings. That was the easy part," Woods said. The hard part was determining how to locate and create the mirror-like polished stone, how to engrave the names and how to install the granite.

"The initial design was more of an idea," said Bill Lecky of the Cooper-Lecky architectural firm. "The actual details— how long the walls were, how many names were on each panel—came out of the [design-build] process."

The challenges that needed to be addressed were numerous. Working with the selected construction contractor, Gilbane Building Company, Cooper-Lecky had to locate the appropriate type of granite: a flawless, reflective, deep ebony stone. "We went on a worldwide search for black granite," Lecky said. "We uncovered five potential stones. One in Bolivia was believed to be too soft. One in Canada was not black enough. One in South Africa was rejected for political rea-

sons. That left one in Sweden and one in India which were felt to be acceptable."

After bids were received from both, the quarry in India was selected. One of the requirements for the project was that the mine could not use explosives to extract the stone, because Cooper-Lecky did not want to risk having it be cracked and flawed. "I have these images of boulders the size of an SUV being dragged out of the mine before being shipped to Baltimore and New York, then trucked to Barre, Vermont, where the stones were cut and polished," Lecky said.

In addition to locating the stone, Cooper-Lecky needed to design the Memorial to be accessible to people with disabilities, calculating just the right angle of the slope. It was set at a 5 percent slope, the maximum allowed without requiring handrails. The architects also needed to determine the size of each granite panel, the size of the lettering and the height of spacing between the lines of names. "If you increase the letter size by one-eighth of an inch, all of a sudden, The Wall gets 25 feet longer," said Lecky. "We performed a graphic analysis to determine how big and how tall the walls needed to be." Ultimately, one of the greatest challenges was how to get that many names on the wall panels in such a short period of time.

(Previous page) Lighting installed after the dedication makes it easier to see the names at night.

(Right) A concrete retaining wall was put up first to support the granite panels of The Wall.

William Lecky

(Top) Names are engraved on one of the panels.

(Left) Panels are set in place against the concrete.

(Background) The Wall as it appeared during construction.

INSCRIBING THE NAMES

"**M**aya Lin's idea was to have all of the names individually hand-chiseled in the stone," explained Bob Doubek. "One stone carver estimated that it would take every craftsman in the world three years and $10 million to do that." Together, the Memorial Fund and Cooper-Lecky searched for a way for the names to be sandblasted rather than hand carved. They needed to figure out how to make stencils for the names and find a sandblasting technique that would not damage the granite.

In August 1982, the Memorial Fund received a call from Larry Century, a young inventor from Cleveland, Ohio, who had read about Maya Lin's design and had devised a process that could be used to inscribe the names. The Memorial Fund sent him some designs and stone, to see if he could do a sample. They came back perfectly designed. Century was selected to serve as a consultant to Binswanger Glass Company in Memphis, Tenn., which was awarded the contract for inscribing the names.

The process began with a photo-positive image of the names, printed on transparent paper, one for each panel. A liquid solution resembling mustard was spread evenly onto a panel and allowed to harden. The photo-positive of the names was mounted on top of the hardened solution, which operated much like photographic print paper. The panel was then rolled into a light booth and blasted with an intense amount of light. Once the panel was wheeled out of the booth, the photo-positive was removed, and the panel was hosed off with water. The "mustard" solution would melt away wherever the names appeared in the photo-positive, leaving sharp, clean-edged letters which looked as if they had been cut out with an X-Acto knife blade. The panels were then sandblasted with aluminum oxide and sand. Once the blasting was completed, the panels were delicately wiped with bleach to remove any remnants of the matrix, leaving the polished granite panels with beautifully etched names.

Initially, the process required a few refinements. "When we did the first few panels, they looked great," Lecky recalled. "Then we asked them to move the panels out into the sun. When we saw them in the sun they were disastrous. You could see these rivers of shadows running through the names. It was clear that the blasting had not been done evenly, with some of the letters etched deeply into the stone, while others were very lightly embossed." To ensure that the sandblasting step was done with even amounts of pressure and force, the team designed a spray booth with a rolling guide, constructed with a series of holes. The sandblasting nozzle was placed through the upper hole of the guide, then rolled evenly and smoothly across a panel. Workers would walk back and forth, moving the nozzle to each subsequent hole, being careful to maintain the same measured pace. The process continued through the lowest and last hole, ensuring a consistent blasting depth over the entire panel. Once in place, the process, though crude, worked to perfection.

The panels that had been scrapped were rolled into a remote corner of the facility where the work was being done, so progress could continue. Years later, rumor spread that a panel from The Wall was for sale on eBay. Apparently, after the owner of the facility died, an abandoned panel was discovered and put up on the auction site. The Memorial Fund contacted eBay, which refused to remove it, and then the owner's son-in-law, who put the panel up for auction. The son-in-law removed the panel from the auction site. It now resides in the Memorial Fund headquarters in Washington, D.C.

The first panel is placed on the Memorial and unveiled on July 22, 1982. Jan Scruggs stands at the podium. At far right is retired chaplain James Kingsley; beside him is Vietnam veteran Congressman John Murtha (D-Pa.). Standing to the right of the panel is Gold Star Mother Emogene Cupp.

Granite panels are shown during the fabrication process in Barre, Vermont.

William Lecky

WALKING THE WALL

"When we were first working on the design, we had no idea it was going to draw the number of people to the site that it does," Lecky explained. "We envisioned people, tourists, walking around with kids, coming across The Wall in the park."

The design intention was for The Wall to rise up seamlessly from the grass, so there were no real provisions for a walkway. However, members of the design team did attempt to address the issue of storm drainage. They designed a sophisticated system which enabled rain to collect and travel down a concrete trough that ran the length of the walls. Narrow concrete slabs with open slats were laid on top of the trough, allowing water to drop down between the slats and drain away.

"The night before the dedication ceremonies, we had two inches of rain," remembered Lecky. "The Memorial looked great the next day; the grass was so lush and green. But when a quarter of a million people showed up, it became a mud bath." All of the grass died, and soon afterward, the Cooper-Lecky team realized that the sophisticated drainage system had not been installed correctly. All of the turf had to be ripped up and the system reinstalled.

During the ceremonies, the team also noticed that visitors to The Wall often stood on top of the drainage slabs as they tried to get close enough to touch the names. But that narrow slab was not sufficient to accommodate foot traffic, nor could the grass withstand it. As a result, when the drainage system was redone, a temporary wooden walkway was erected to meet the needs of visitors better. Even still, within weeks, it became obvious that traffic at The Wall was going to be much higher than anyone had anticipated. Cooper-Lecky began planning and reworking the paths.

"There were so many people coming. In no time, the National Park Service put up a black chain-link fence so people couldn't walk on the grass," Lecky recalled. "But a few months after the dedication, they called to ask us to widen the path. A few months later, they needed to widen it again."

Crowds weren't the only surprise. In the early months of The Wall, there were also many threats to damage and vandalize the Memorial. A group of Vietnam veterans began to camp voluntarily on its grounds, in accordance with National Park Service (NPS) rules, in order to stand guard and protect The Wall.

One night, James "J.C." Cummings, a young architect on the Cooper-Lecky design team, headed down to the site to handle some business. Dusk had melted into darkness. As he made his way to The Wall, a gruff man approached him and sternly asked what he was doing. Cummings explained who he was and why he was there. The veteran's manner softened, and he asked Cummings if he wanted to be escorted to The Wall. Cummings declined, but as he got closer to the Memorial, he noticed another veteran holding a lantern, escorting a visitor to a name. As the veteran and visitor walked The Wall, the lantern swung gently left to right. Cummings noticed the swinging lantern poignantly reflected in the blackness of The Wall.

"This particular image was the very expression of 'service.' These individuals [were] protecting The Wall, escorting visitors to it, caring for it with such love, and The Wall was reflecting all of that beauty," he explained. For Cummings, that vision captured all that The Wall was intended to be. "I don't know if I'll ever see something that clearly again," he added. Cummings has been the architect of record for The Wall since 1997.

Lighting the Way

It was always hoped that the Memorial would be accessible to visitors 24 hours a day. For two years, volunteer veterans kept a nighttime vigil to light the way for visitors, until a lighting system was installed in 1984. At the time, the lighting system was state-of-the-art. However, it required a fair amount of maintenance. Lights were set into the ground near the base of The Wall, and water would leak into various components. Because it was a custom-built system, the replacement parts and bulbs were difficult to order.

By 2004, after 20 years, it was time to update the lighting. An extensive study was conducted to design a system that would be both easier to maintain and would enhance the nighttime experiences at The Wall. The new lighting system was paid for by the Memorial Fund.

Some of the new lighting was to be set into the paving. But it was discovered that the giant concrete drainage trench had not only twisted, it had also settled and sunk several inches. Replacement drainage and paving systems were necessary. To protect the walls from errant equipment and flying debris, they had to be covered completely during the repairs. Work was done on one side and then the other, so that the entire Memorial did not have to be closed to the public.

During the construction process, as crews hoisted the old pavers, they discovered hundreds of small objects that had been left at The Wall and had fallen through the paving joints. "It was a very moving situation," Cummings recalled. "Something as ordinary as picking up a sidewalk led to finding all of those items." There were notes, religious medals, rings and trinkets. Each day, workers took great care to retrieve the items so they could be catalogued and added to the greater collection.

Reconditioning of the lights and improvements to the paving and walkway took place in 1992 for the 10th anniversary of The Wall.

(All photos this page by William Lecky)

Jim Bannion

Daniel Arant

New lighting was installed in 2004, featuring
lights that sit flush to the ground.

Volunteer Leroy Lawson talks
with active duty soldiers.

Families are among the many volunteers who come to wash The Wall.

CARING FOR THE WALL

Today, The Wall has a host of people and organizations that care about and for it. The National Park Service is its legal steward, while the Memorial Fund makes significant contributions to assist in its care. "The volunteers at The Wall are the 'first responders,'" Cummings explained. They are intimately familiar with the Memorial and are usually the first to notice when there may be a problem. When they do, they inform NPS or the Memorial Fund, so that a convention of caregivers can meet to determine the best solution.

The Memorial Fund provides insurance for The Wall. In 2004, it paid more than $1 million to install the new lighting system. Annually, the Memorial Fund also pays to have names inscribed on The Wall. In these ways, the Memorial Fund has shared maintenance responsibilities with the National Park Service in a model public/private partnership.

A detailed care manual developed by Cooper-Lecky guides most of the general maintenance. Since the majority of the Memorial is a park setting, much of the maintenance involves lawn care. One year, dandelions threatened to take over the entire grounds. For the Three Servicemen, NPS waxes the statue each Memorial Day and Veterans Day to protect its bronze finish.

The National Park Service organizes and schedules weekly washings of The Wall by groups of volunteers, from April to November when the temperatures are above freezing. The groups consist of student, veteran, civic and community organizations from a variety of locations. Groups contact NPS during the winter in order to secure a date and be placed on the 31-week schedule. On Wall washing day, which is typically a Saturday or Sunday, volunteers meet at The Wall between 6:00 and 6:30 in the morning. A ranger provides them with brooms, hoses, trash bags, nozzles and a brief instructional safety talk. Usually, groups are made up of 10 to 15 people, although on occasion they may be as large as 40.

A few years after the Korean Memorial was completed, it too needed some love and care. On their own, some groups of volunteers have gone to the Korean Memorial to clean it, once they were done at The Wall. To Cummings, the tender care that spilled over to the Korean Memorial demonstrates the powerful, positive impact The Wall has had on its surrounding neighborhood and the community.

(Right) A National Park Service employee washes The Wall.

Members of Vietnam Veterans of America Chapter 641, from Silver Spring, Md., wash The Wall on the first Saturday of every month, April through November.

Daniel Arant

Daniel Arant

J.C. Cummings (right), architect of record for the Vietnam Veterans Memorial, leads a tour at The Wall for educators during the 2007 Teach Vietnam Teachers Network National Conference.

Volunteer William Harris helps visitors find the names of loved ones.

Leroy Lawson

Smithsonian

WALL MAGIC

THE SEARCH FOR A NAME COMES FULL CIRCLE
BY
ARTHUR DRESCHER

On St. Patrick's Day 1973, I met a young woman at a church retreat, and it was special from the moment we met. Her name was Barbara and she lived in Washington, D.C. At the time we met, she was wearing an MIA bracelet for Brian Kent McGar. I didn't know it at the time, but that the bracelet would play an important part in my life more than 20 years later.

It was a whirlwind courtship. We got engaged on June 10 and were married on August 4.

By 1978, we were the proud parents of two sons. Although we lived in Philadelphia, we visited friends and spent time in Washington whenever we could. After the Vietnam Memorial was built in 1982, we would make sure to visit. We tried to find the name from Barbara's bracelet on The Wall, but we could not remember how it was spelled, and we never located it.

Barbara died of breast cancer in September 1986. She never got to see Brian McGar's name on The Wall. But, my sons and I continued to visit Washington, and on one of our visits to The Wall, we found the name. Somehow, it almost felt that Barbara was there, too.

In 1995, on a visit to The Wall, I heard a volunteer couple tell a visitor that they came for a week once or twice a year to work there. That got me to thinking that I could be a volunteer, too.

I worked at The Wall for the first time in December 1996, a helping visitors like others had helped my sons and me. It was all I had hoped the experience would be, and more. I found myself driving to Washington as often as I could to work. I sometimes joke that my new wife, Bonnie, would be a "Wall Widow" on weekends if we lived closer to D.C.

In the summer of 2002, I met a social studies teacher from California named Marilyn Wood while I was volunteering at The Wall, and I told her about the Memorial Fund's Teach Vietnam Teachers Network national conference. The first one was held in 2002, over the very week she was visiting. We exchanged e-mail addresses and communicated several times over the next year. The following spring, I found out she would be coming to the 2003 Teachers Conference.

One of the only assignments each teacher had been given before the conference was to find the name of someone on The Wall who had a connection to them and then honor that person the last night of the conference. On the first afternoon of the 2003 conference, a volunteer friend told me he had met Marilyn at The Wall that day. She was working on the computer just then, so I went over to greet her. As I approached, I saw on the screen the name of Brian Kent McGar. I was astonished and asked her why she was looking up information about him. I had never told her about my wife's MIA bracelet. Marilyn told me that she had gone to high school with him, and she was presently teaching in that high school in Ceres, Calif.

I couldn't believe what she had just told me. I had invited a complete stranger to come to the conference, and out of more than 58,000 names on The Wall, she knew Brian McGar and his family. Amazing!

During the course of the week, Marilyn and I got to know each other better, and she was able to give me information her local paper had printed in stories over the years concerning Brian.

So, 30 years after I met that girl who was wearing an MIA bracelet with Brian McGar's name on it, that part of my life has come full circle. Brian Kent McGar is no longer just a name on The Wall. And, I still have the bracelet.

Brian Kent McGar had his status updated from MIA to KIA on Panel 21E, Line 23 on The Wall.

Arthur Drescher lives in Glenside, Pa., and continues to volunteer at The Wall.

Visitors to The Wall often make name rubbings.

Leroy Lawson

52

CHAPTER 3
THE NAMES

Daniel Arant

RICHARD A CASSIN
...DER FORE
THOMAS M JAGGERS
...AM
...DERICK A McMAHON
...OD C SOVEY Jr
...ARD K WHITFIELD
MARTIN CAVAZOS
...MANNION
CARL F PEPPLE Jr
...LIP L ROUSE
...MAS
...WOODS
...C ELLERBROCK
...AND
...RT C REYNOLDS
...OMAS C EVANS

JAMES W ROBBINS
MICHAEL SESSA Jr
CALVIN L TAYLOR
ROBERT A TURNER
RICHARD K GILLIN...
ANTON T BORNST...
WILLIAM J CORBIN
REYNALDO SALIN...
RAMON GONZAL...
HAROLD J HELLBA...
WILLIAM D JINKS
CHARLES W LARN...
JAMES M MOSGR...
JAMES K PATTERS...
THOMAS A RON...
ALTON SHEDD...
MARTIN N TULL...

THE NAMES

"**R**hythmic Spanish names. Tongue-twisting Polish names, guttural German, exotic African, homely Anglo-Saxon names," wrote *Newsweek* editor-in-chief William Broyles, who served in Vietnam as a Marine infantry lieutenant. "Chinese, Polynesian, Indian, and Russian names. They are names which run deep into the heart of America, each testimony to a family's decision, sometime in the past, to wrench itself from home and culture to test our country's promise of new opportunities and a better life. They are names drawn from the farthest corners of the world and then, in this generation, sent to another distant corner in a war America has done its best to forget. But to hear the names being read...is to remember. The war was about names, each name a special human being who never came home."

When The Wall was dedicated in 1982, there were 57,939 names inscribed. Approximately 1,300 names are of servicemen who were either missing or prisoners of war.

The essence of The Wall is the names and the reaction of the visitor to seeing his or her reflection in this sea of remembrance. Millions more come to experience this Memorial each year. Some are drawn to The Wall like pilgrims to Mecca. Others think it is just another tourist stop until they feel the haunting power of this unique work of remembrance designed by Maya Lin, a 21-year-old American.

James "J.C." Cummings, architect of record for The Wall, remembered when the impact of seeing all of the names collectively first dawned on him. He was visiting the site during construction after the first panel had been installed. "Seeing the expanse of the concrete retaining wall was impressive," Cummings recalled. "There was one piece of granite held in place. It seemed as if it was suspended in air, all on its own."

Cummings approached the panel. He had been busy for weeks proofreading names for the engraving templates, so it was a natural reflex for him to begin reading the names at the top of the panel. As he read name after name, he finally reached the line at eye level and realized that he had grown tired from reading the names. "That's when I realized how vast the actual number of names would be and how many lives were lost," he said.

(This page, above and at right) People of all ages come to visit The Wall, and emotions are often visible.

(Previous page) A dog tag is left between the panels of The Wall.

1959

IN H■N■R ■F THE MEN AND W■MEN ■F THE ARMED F■R■ES ■F THE UNITED STATES WH■ SERVED IN THE VIETNAM WAR. THE NAMES ■F TH■SE WHO GAVE THEIR LIVES AND OF THOSE WHO REMAIN MISSING ARE INSCRIBED IN THE ORDER THEY WERE TAKEN FROM US.

DALE R BUIS • CHESTER N OVNARD • MAURICE W FLOURNOY • ALFONS A BANKWOSKI • FREDERICK T GARSIDE •
RALPH W MAGEE • GLENN MATTESON • LESLIE V SAMPSON • EDGAR W WEITKAMP Jr • OSCAR B WESTIN Jr •
THEODORE G FELAND • GERALD M BIBER • JOHN M BISCHOFF • ODIS D ARNOLD • WALTER H MOON •
BRUCE R JONES • FLOYD STUDER • JAMES T DAVIS • HERMAN K DURRWACHTER Jr • FRED M STEUER • TOM J CRESS •
THEODORE J BERLETT • MILO B COGHILL • FERGUS C GROVES II • ROBERT D LARSON • JOSEPH M FAHEY Jr •
FLOYD M FRAZIER • STANLEY G HARTSON • EDWARD K KISSAM Jr • JACK D LE TOURNEAU • GLEN F MERRIHEW •
LEWIS M WALLING Jr • ROBERT L WESTFALL • CHARLES A PULLIAM • AL SUMINGGUIT PADAYHAG •
■■AN P WHITLOCK • MILTON D BRITTON • BARNEY KAATZ • JAMES GABRIEL Jr • WAYNE E MARCHAND •
BILLIE L BEARD • RONALD E LEWIS • HEWETT E COE • GEORGE E COLLIER • ROBERT L GARDNER •
WALTER R McCARTHY Jr • WILLIAM F TRAIN III • ROBERT L SIMPSON • DON J YORK • JOSEPH A GOLDBERG •
HAROLD L GUTHRIE • JAMES E LANE • ANTHONY J TENCZA • WILLIAM R BUNKER III • RICHARD L K ELLIS •
THOMAS E ANDERSON • GERALD C GRIFFIN • RICHARD E HAMILTON • GERALD O NORTON • JERALD W PENDELL •
MICHAEL J TUNNEY • MIGUEL A VALENTIN Jr • HERBERT W BOOTH Jr • TERRY D CORDELL • RICHARD L FOXX •
JOHNNIE GENE LEE • GARRY C McFETRIDGE • ROBERT D BENNETT • WILLIAM B TULLY • RICHARD D BENZEL •
CHARLES E HOLLOWAY • JACK M LISLE • DONALD L BRAMAN • WILLIAM L DEAL • KENNETH N GOOD •
CLAYTON A FANNIN • CHARLES M FITTS • LAWRENCE C HAMMOND • BOYCE E LAWSON • JAMES D McANDREW •
LEWIS L STONE • DONALD B TOTH • RAYMOND C WILDE • JOHN DUARTE • LEON J KRAMER • RICHARD E STEPHAN •
JOHN P BARTLEY • JOHN F SHAUGHNESSY Jr • JAMES R O'NEILL • BERNARD L GRAY • ROBERT BURGERT •
■RAIG B WOLFORD • CHARLES W McCARY • ODES W JEFFERS • JAMES H ISHIHARA • DAVID WEBSTER •
■ALTER P GORHAM • FLOYD R DAVIS • JIMMY R GRIFFIN • LAVESTER L WILLIAMS • ANDREW C MITCHELL III •
JERRY A CAMPAIGNE • RAMOND E DOYLE • RICHARD L HATLESTAD • STANLEY E TRUESDALE • RUBE A FREEMAN •
PARKER D CRAMER • ROBERT J MAIN • JAMES A ELLIS • JOHN C MYATT • CHARLES E DOERRMAN • ROBERT J HAIN •
JAMES H BRODT • NEIL K MacIVER • HOWARD M EAKIN Jr • CHARLES B JOHNSON Jr • PERCY W HOWELL •
G W MAGBEE • CONDON H TERRY • CURTIS J STECKBAUER • RICHARD W GEYER • PAUL R SMITH •
RAYMOND F PARKS • CARL H BALLARD • JACK L GOODMAN • LAWRENCE E HACKLEY • ROBERT K MOSIER •
CLARENCE C TESSMAN • DONALD V McGREGOR • ARTHUR E BEDAL • JOHN H McCLEAN • DONALD G LOGAN •
CLAUDE W McBRIDE • EDWARD B CRIBB • ARCHIE S BOWEN • TIMOTHY M LANG • JAMES E WENZEL •

Panel 1 East begins the chronological listing of the names.

THE ORDER OF NAMES

After Lin's design was selected, one of the early debates was whether the names should appear on The Wall in alphabetical or chronological order. Lin's intention from the beginning was to have the names appear chronologically, beginning and ending at the apex. She wanted the names to tell the journey, or the timeline, of the war. This approach would allow veterans, friends and family members to find a loved one by his or her date of casualty. It would also enable veterans to find groups of friends who died during the same incident. Fallen comrades could be together on The Wall, as they'd been in death. And there would be nothing to denote service or rank. No single person's service or sacrifice would be any greater than anyone else's. All would be represented equally, with generals listed alongside infantrymen.

Lin's vision prevailed. The names are listed in chronological order, according to the date of casualty. This is "the genius of Maya's design," said Scruggs.

"The chronological order allows veterans who were in a battle to see their friends forever united on The Wall," he explained. "As she wisely predicted, this would help bring the veterans back in time—and a cathartic healing would occur for many by facing this loss again."

Scruggs also pointed out that some common names appear on the Memorial more than once. Chronological order by date of casualty allows friends and family members to pick out their loved one from all of the others with the same name.

The casualty date is the date the person was killed or wounded in combat or injured during an accident; for the missing, the date is when the person was reported missing. The first two names listed on Panel 1, East Wall, at the apex are from July 8, 1959. On that panel, above the names is this inscription:

In honor of the men and women of the armed forces of the United States who served in the Vietnam War. The names of those who gave their lives and of those who remain missing are inscribed in the order they were taken from us.

The last 18 names listed on the bottom of Panel 1, West Wall, also at the apex, are from May 15, 1975. These names are followed by the inscription:

Our nation honors the courage, sacrifice and devotion to duty and country of its Vietnam veterans. This memorial was built with private contributions from the American people. November 11, 1982.

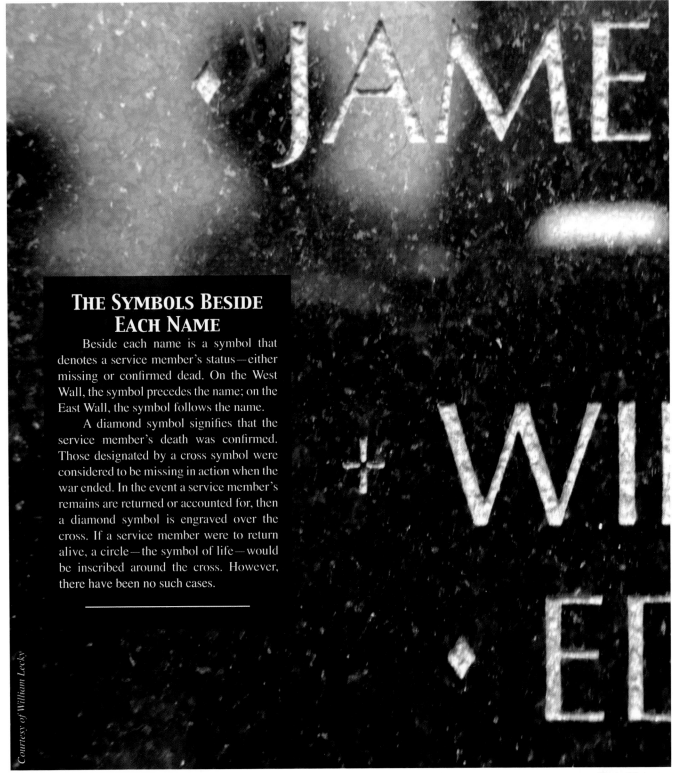

Courtesy of William Lecky

THE SYMBOLS BESIDE EACH NAME

Beside each name is a symbol that denotes a service member's status—either missing or confirmed dead. On the West Wall, the symbol precedes the name; on the East Wall, the symbol follows the name.

A diamond symbol signifies that the service member's death was confirmed. Those designated by a cross symbol were considered to be missing in action when the war ended. In the event a service member's remains are returned or accounted for, then a diamond symbol is engraved over the cross. If a service member were to return alive, a circle—the symbol of life—would be inscribed around the cross. However, there have been no such cases.

JAMES V DRAGONE · DALE E SHULTZ · MICHA
N G BUCHANAN · PAUL J DAMATO Jr · SAMUEL E DICK ·
· LARRY M HEEN · ALBRO L LUNDY Jr · CALVIN D MACK ·
HAEL R NUGENT · VERN E ODOM Jr · WESLEY L PHILLIPS ·
PENCE Jr · MICHAEL J TECCO · WILLIAM H YOUNT Jr · TH
CKERBOCKER · ANTHONY A BRESE · RICHARD W DOTSO
JOHNSON · MARSHALL MILLER · MICHAEL D McADOO
LOBOS · LAWRENCE G BANGS · RAYMOND R COOREM
YMOND C HOLT · ROY D JORDAN · JACK W McCANN ·
TEMPLETON · CARVER J VAUGHAN · JERRY E HANCOCK
· KENNETH W GRIFFIN · JAMES L SMITH · ROGER L TEETE
HY H LACY · JOHN E NORTON · HOWARD W BRAMLETT
RIAN A HORINEK · LARRY J ANDERSON · HAROLD E ASHE
· JERRY B EDMONDS Jr · RICHARD MEDINA ESCALERA ·
N · IRA E GIBBS · LEROY E HALBERT Jr · STEVE L J LAVERTY ·
STON C ROBERTS · WAYNE S RUSHTON · ALFREDO SALA
N WEBSTER · FREDERICK R FRACIONE · THOMAS H HUD
EUGENE I SMITH · DONALD D WINN · STANLEY G CROC
KITSCH Jr · RAMON A SERVERA BAEZ · HARVEY G SOKOL
UCE M KELLER · HARRY LEWIS Jr · PATRICK J MAGEE · TH
NIS W OMELIA · CARL A PALEN · MICHAEL D PARSONS
EE STERN · WILLIAM T STODARD · CHARLES W STRATTO
· ROBERT A DOTEN · GLEN C KLEIN · BRIAN R KOEHN · B
R Jr · DONALD M CRAMER · RAYMOND R ENYEART Jr · H
LENN E KELLY · DOUGLAS B KENT · JOHN W LYNCH III ·
NIE V ROGERS · GLENN C VALENTE · FREDERICK W BALD
CE L GOODSELL · STEVEN MIKE · CARLETON P MILLER Jr
5 · RICK S BROWN · GERARD CORRIVEAU · JAMES L CRA
ERT B MICHALK · RUSSEL C NELSON · ROBERT L PAYNTE
ABOR · WILLIAM C VASEY · DOUGLAS M BECKMAN · JA
RRY · ROBERT DEGEN · ROBERT D DUFF · BILLY W HARTV
DY · CECIL C OLSEN · JAMES R SHAW · JOHN E STEWART
BENNIE F JONES · DAVID W LILLEY · LOUIS PAYNE Sr · CL
N L WIRTH Jr · WILLARD E WOODY · BARRY H BERGER ·
· DOUGLAS O FORD · LEWIS S HALL · JERRY T HICKEY ·
G · JOE H LILLIE · CORNELIUS H RAM · JACKIE LEE SAWN
ROBERT D BLACK Jr · RICHARD V BLACKBURN · LEE W C
INS · THOMAS F IRVIN · WILLIAM F JOHNSON · DAVID
SANDOVAL · WILLIE STRACNER · FRANCIS J THORP
HENDRI W HOWARD KAPUSTA · BILLY RAY PRICE Jr ·

Tom Estrin

SELECTING NAMES FOR THE WALL

Bob Doubek, a veteran and founding member of the Memorial Fund, was tasked with identifying all of the names to be included on The Wall. During and after the Vietnam War, the Department of Defense (DOD) compiled a list of combat zone casualties according to criteria in a 1965 Presidential Executive Order. It specified the geographic areas of Vietnam, Laos, Cambodia and surrounding coastal areas as combat zones. If a person died or went missing in those areas, DOD considered that individual to be a combat zone casualty and eligible for inclusion on The Wall.

Unfortunately, the Department of Defense and the individual service branches maintained separate casualty lists with differing criteria. This was long before the advent of integrated computer databases. The result: no comprehensive master list of Vietnam War casualties existed. Getting the individual branches to cross-reference their information with the DOD list would be impossible. That job would instead fall to Doubek.

Compounding these difficulties was the issue that many casualties, particularly from the Air Force, were not always straightforward in terms of locale. "In order to have your name on The Wall, you had to have died within the 'war zone,'" explained Doubek. "But you had stories of guys in the Air Force who would die in their aircraft over Thailand after having been shot over Vietnam." Technically, they were ineligible for inclusion on The Wall.

For those and a handful of other unique circumstances, Doubek made his own list of men who had died due to their combat experiences—names that may have been listed by an individual service branch, but not by DOD. With this list in hand, he went to the various locations where individual service records were kept, pulling and reviewing each file.

"I looked at the record to determine whether mortal wounds were sustained," Doubek said of the service members whose names were listed by the individual service branches, but not by DOD. He added that he tried to make the best call he could when adding names to the list. Unfortunately, a small number of names of men who were still alive were mistakenly added to The Wall. To put a circle around the symbol beside their names would not provide the correct historical context related to their situation. Their names, however, have been removed from the printed *Directory of Names*.

In addition to making sure the list of names was inclusive, another challenge was ensuring the accuracy of the names. Doubek contacted the National Personnel Records Center, Archives and Records Service in St. Louis, Mo. On the other end of that phone call was an Air Force officer who had served in Vietnam. He would become instrumental in helping Doubek identify names and check spellings.

Once a master list was compiled, the names were checked manually for errors. "We worked very hard with volunteers from the Gold Star Mothers," recalled Doubek. For weeks and weeks, a team worked through the list, verifying spellings and ensuring that the computer printout that was to be used for the stenciling was correct.

During one review, Doubek found a glitch with the computer software: it did not recognize the spaces that appeared within a last name, such as "van der Meide." It could not properly denote a generational suffix, nor could it discern between a compounded first name, such as Billy Bob, vs. a traditional first and middle name. As a result, the software improperly truncated or abbreviated names. With the glitch discovered, Doubek and his team located and hand-corrected each error.

On the stencil printouts, each line contained five names per row. In some instances, names needed to be shuffled in order to fit on a line. Or, if a name was particularly long, it would be swapped with a shorter name. "I went through the whole list of names eight times, because I was concerned about the correct formatting," remembered Doubek.

Such a painstaking effort colored Doubek's early experiences at the Memorial. "I would say that I am one of the [few] people who is least affected by The Wall emotionally," he said. "I know where all the cracks are, where all the misspellings and mistakes are. But within the first two years after its dedication, I began to read all of these great things about it in the press, and then I was gratified."

(Left) The Washington Monument's reflection on The Wall is a favorite shot for photographers.

(Opposite page, top) Stoneworkers measure the depth of the lettering of a new name being added to The Wall.

(Bottom left) Jan Scruggs watches as Robert Rumley's name is inscribed.

(Bottom right) Mark Rumley touches his brother's name after it is added to The Wall.

THE ADDITION OF NAMES

By 2007, a total of 317 names had been added since The Wall's dedication. There are now 58,256 names. The first group, added in 1983, included 68 Marines who were killed when their R&R (rest and relaxation) flight crashed in Hong Kong. A few years after the dedication, the issue of geographic criteria was expanded by DOD to include people who had been killed outside of the war zone while on or in support of direct combat missions. This change prompted the addition of 110 names in 1986.

The Vietnam Veterans Memorial Fund receives numerous requests each year from individuals who wish to have particular names added to the Memorial. While the Memorial Fund finances the name additions to The Wall, it is the Department of Defense that makes these difficult and often technical decisions. The Memorial Fund does not have the authority to overrule those who adjudicate these matters. *(For information on where to address name addition requests, see Appendix 4.)*

Once additions are approved by DOD, the Memorial Fund receives the list of approved names, coordinates the inscribing and absorbs the costs.

Names that become eligible for inclusion are added once each year, in May, a few weeks before Memorial Day. Family members are invited to witness the inscription and also to at-tend the annual Memorial Day ceremony when the new names are read at The Wall.

For families who have worked to have their loved one's name added, the journey can be long and exhausting. Some have tried for years before receiving approval from DOD. Colleen Pontes, whose father Kevin Joyce was added in 2003, remembered the rush of emotions she felt as she and her brother watched their dad's name being inscribed in the granite. "Proving a direct correlation to the injuries is a challenge," Pontes explained. "I respect the process, but it can be hard to prove something that's in your heart."

"That's what makes it so special when you see the name going up," she added. "And they are so respectful when they do the engraving. They seem honored to be putting the names on The Wall."

Jim Lee, formerly of Great Panes Glassworks and now with Engrave Write in Denver, comes every year to add the names to The Wall. Lee sets the artwork, finds places in the margins where each name can fit, tries hard to put each name among comrades and is careful to create a mockup which closely resembles the style and depth of the other names. "They do a really good job making the physical appearance of the names match the original panel," Cummings noted.

VVMF

ADDING A NAME TO THE WALL:
ROBERT PATRICK RUMLEY JR.

During the Vietnam War, the use of helicopters enabled many service members who had been wounded to receive medical attention sooner than they would have otherwise. It allowed them to be airlifted to safety. This dramatically increased the number of service members who were able to survive their wounds and injuries. A total of 304,000 people were wounded, with 75,000 being severely disabled, suffering amputations or crippling injuries. Sadly, while the injured returned home, it didn't mean they were all able to reclaim life. Many died days, weeks, months and even years later, as a direct result of their wounds.

This was the case for Capt. Robert Patrick Rumley Jr., USMC. Bobby, as his family called him, was the second child and oldest son of Beatrice and Robert Rumley's seven children. An Irish Catholic family from Medford, Mass., the Rumleys have a long history of military service for their country.

Bobby went to Vietnam in the spring of 1966. On Sept. 2, a helicopter carrying him and his platoon was shot down. Although Bobby was rescued, he never recovered from his injuries.

For months, he was treated at Chelsea Naval Hospital in Boston. Pain in his left hip made it difficult for him to walk. Then, he suffered a series of seizures and debilitating paralysis that robbed him of his mobility, one limb at a time. In early 1968, he was transferred to Faulkner Hospital, also in Boston, where he lay comatose and unresponsive. On May 18, 1968, 20 months after his helicopter went down, Bobby died from a brain tumor believed to have resulted from the head trauma he experienced during the crash.

"Watching Bobby go from a vibrant, aggressive 185-pound, reasonably good athlete to a 60-pound bag of bones, which is what he looked like on the morning of May 18, 1968, was a life altering experience," his brother Mike explained.

The pain of his loss was magnified years later when they discovered that Bobby's name was not included on The Wall. "When The Wall was being built, there was a listing of the names in the newspaper," Mike Rumley remembered. "We were looking for his name and couldn't find it. We were devastated. Our expectations were that he would go on The Wall. There was no reason to think otherwise."

Years passed. Often, friends would ask the Rumleys why Bobby's name was not on The Wall. They didn't have an answer. Several of the Rumley children contemplated petitioning to have his name added, but reconsidered, believing that their parents did not want to wage a fight.

In July 2004, Mike's wife Martha learned of a person at Marine Casualty Division at Quantico, Va., whose job it was to receive petitions regarding Marines and The Wall. With his parents deceased, Mike felt comfortable pursuing the issue. He encouraged his brother Mark, the lawyer in the family, to spearhead a petition to have Bobby's name added.

Mark went to work amassing stacks of military papers and documentation of Bobby's injuries and related care. Their challenge: to prove that Bobby's death was the direct result of the injuries he suffered. One of their first calls was to Massachusetts Congressman Edward Markey, who immediately offered his support.

"When Michael and I put the original petition together in August 2004, we both thought it would be a slam dunk," Mark remembered. "All of the records were there, and we did comparisons to other cases. We thought we'd hear in a few months and that would be it. Months went on, and we didn't hear anything." In 2005, they received a call notifying them that their request had been denied.

But they were not deterred. For the next several months, they strategized daily on how they could push the petition through to approval. Mark scrutinized the paperwork until he found the key they needed: It was a transfer approval for their brother Stephen, who had also served in Vietnam. During his second tour, shortly after Bobby died, he had requested a transfer to the United States. At the time, a service member could request a transfer if he had a mother, father, brother or sister who died as a result of serving in Vietnam. Stephen's request had been approved.

For Mark, the approved transfer proved that the military acknowledged Bobby's death as the result of his service in Vietnam. "My argument was: 'You approved this in the past, you have to approve this again,'" he explained.

After submitting some additional documentation, the Rumley family received a phone call just before Thanksgiving 2005, confirming that Congressman Markey had spoken with Brig. Gen. Michael Downs, USMC (Ret.), who had approved the petition. By February, DOD had rendered its approval.

On May 18, 2006, 38 years to the day that Bobby Rumley died, his family watched as the name Robert Patrick Rumley Jr. was added to The Wall. (Panel 14E, Row 95.)

(Previous page) Stephen, Mark and Michael Rumley stand by their brother's name.

Veterans look up a name in the directory.

Volunteer Annmarie Emmet looks for a name.

Leroy Lawson

Donna Prince

The directory helps visitors locate names on The Wall.

LOCATING A NAME

Although the names are not listed alphabetically, it is not difficult for visitors to find a name on the Memorial. The National Park Service offers these steps for locating a name:

1. Look up the name in the Vietnam Veterans Memorial *Directory of Names*. These directories are located at both ends of The Wall and contain an alphabetical listing of all the names on the Memorial.
2. Note the panel and line number for the name listed. The panel number is a number/letter combination, such as 10W or 35E. "W" denotes the west arm of The Wall, and "E" denotes the east arm.
3. Locate the corresponding panel at the Memorial. The west arm of The Wall is on the left when standing at the center facing The Wall. The east arm is the right half. The panels are numbered beginning from the center out toward the ends of The Wall. The panel numbers are inscribed at the bottom of each panel.
4. Locate the line on which the name is inscribed. Count down from the top of the panel. Inscribed dots in the margins of every other panel mark every 10 lines to aid in counting.

National Park Service rangers and volunteers are available to assist in locating names at the Memorial. Names can also be located on The Virtual Wall on the Memorial Fund's Web site, *www.vvmf.org*. *(To purchase a* Directory of Names, *see Appendix 4.)*

A visitor makes a name rubbing.

Tom Estrin

WALL MAGIC

RECONNECTING WITH PEOPLE YOU KNEW
BY
CHARLIE HAROOTUNIAN

On three occasions, I have been at The Wall when visitors have requested name rubbings of people I knew. One was a Marine who asked for the name of a college classmate of mine who took his ROTC commission in the Marine Corps. The classmate and I were in Vietnam at the same time, but he was killed after five days in-country. I always wondered what had happened to him, and this visitor had wondered about him prior to his entering the Corps. We both provided missing pieces to each other.

When you consider the number of people whose names are on The Wall and the number of visitors to The Wall, the odds are extraordinary that we would meet.

On two other occasions, people asked for the same name of one of the men who served in my platoon who was our first casualty. The first visitor was a neighbor and the second was someone who works with one of his brothers. Both provided a wealth of information about the family and their location. What are the odds of that happening once, never mind twice?

On the 20th anniversary of The Wall, all the names were read in chronological order, taking over three days. Many volunteers, family members, veterans and citizens took part in the name reading. On the last day, I was working near the stage when I noticed a regular attendee at the Veterans Day ceremonies standing nearby.

I spoke with him for a while and asked him if he had read any names yet. He said that he had not, and it was just something he could not do. He said he was standing around because there were eight men he had served with whose names are on The Wall and he wanted to be there when their names were being read. Just then, someone came up to me and handed me their list of 30 names and apologized, saying they were to read in about a half hour but could not stay. I said it would not be a problem. There were enough volunteers available so that the names would be covered.

Then I handed the sheet to my friend and said that he was going to read the names. He was hesitant, but accepted the list. After about two minutes, his face had a look of shock. I asked what the matter was. He said that the sheet I had given him had five of the eight names on it.

Wall Magic. What are the odds?

Charlie Harootunian is a Vietnam veteran who has volunteered at The Wall since 1986. He lives in Massachusetts.

Volunteer Charlie Harootunian makes a rubbing.

Daniel Arant

Daniel Arant

A member of a Native American color guard holds a flag near The Wall.

Master Sgt. Jonathan Deutsch, U.S. Army Chorus, often sings the National Anthem at ceremonies.

Daniel Arant © Frederick E. Hart/VVMF, 1984

Leroy Lawson

Mariah Payne

(Top left) The Three Servicemen statue stands guard over The Wall.   (Top right) A father and daughter make a rubbing.   (Above) Early mornings are a quiet time at The Wall.

Daniel Arant © Frederick E. Hart/VVMF, 1984

VVMF © 1993, VVMF; Glenna Goodacre, Sculptor

Daniel Arant © Frederick E. Hart/VVMF, 1984

The Three Servicemen statue and the Vietnam Women's Memorial were added after The Wall was completed.

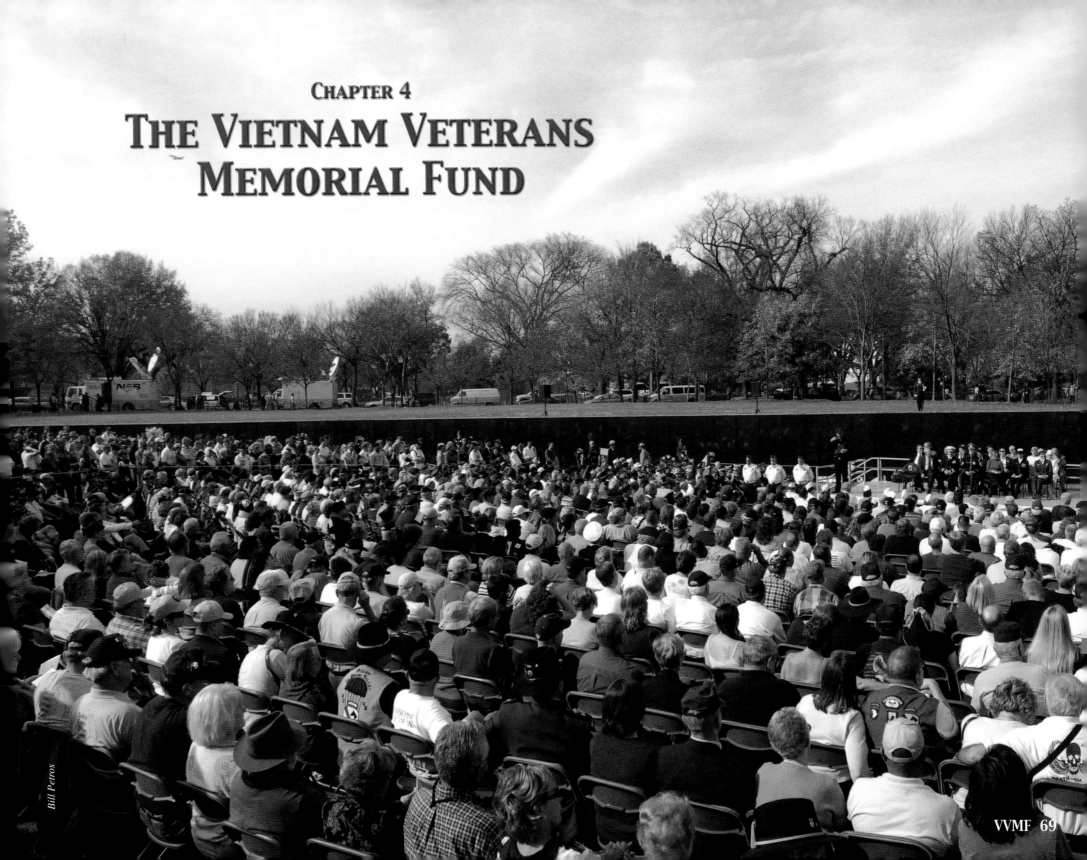

Chapter 4
The Vietnam Veterans Memorial Fund

Bill Petros

Visitors leave a variety of items at The Wall. Most nonperishable items are collected, catalogued and archived at the Museum Resource Center.

THE VIETNAM VETERANS MEMORIAL FUND

The Vietnam Veterans Memorial was initially conceived with one overriding purpose: to bring long overdue honor and recognition to the men and women of the U.S. armed forces who served and sacrificed in Vietnam.

With the dedication complete and the Memorial in the care of the National Park Service, the Memorial Fund had achieved its goals. So, in the years following the dedication, "I started letting all my staff go and told them to go find other, better jobs," recalled Jan Scruggs, founder and president of the Memorial Fund. By February 1985, the Memorial Fund had essentially shut down, although Scruggs, a core group of supporters and the National Park Service organized large ceremonial events at The Wall each Memorial and Veterans Day.

"The assumption was that the Memorial would be like all the rest of the memorials. It would be there, but fade into more of a fraternal monument," he said.

Instead, the Memorial was transcending its role as a national symbol of healing. It was having the unique ability to inspire exploration and reflection about the Vietnam War, a critical time in our nation's past, and enabling Americans to cast a wiser eye toward the future. The items left at The Wall by visitors offered a compelling glimpse at the Memorial's burgeoning impact on society.

Accolades for the Memorial were also on the rise. "One of our board members was in Paris and saw the Memorial profiled in a magazine," remembered Scruggs. "Internationally, it was being recognized as a great work of art. As the significance of it began to grow, we decided to re-form the Memorial Fund in 1991." As the 10th anniversary of The Wall approached, Scruggs and the board of directors saw the need to re-establish the Memorial Fund for the commemorations and renovations that would be taking place in the coming year.

The plan was once again to dismantle the staff after the 10th anniversary, and indeed, this began to happen, with the staff shrinking from nearly 20 to three in the months following the end of the anniversary commemorations. Then, the idea began to develop that there were other objectives the Memorial Fund could pursue besides commemoration. So, instead of shutting down, the Memorial Fund remained open to fulfill a perceived need of the public, for education and healing about the Vietnam War. One of the key employees hired for the 10th anniversary who stayed to usher the Memorial Fund into its new role was Libby Hatch, who remained committed to the Memorial until her death in 1998. A volunteer award given by the Memorial Fund and the Hatch family is named in her honor.

Expectations for the re-established Memorial Fund, Scruggs said, "were to study and use the Memorial in a positive way. We found that this Memorial could do a lot of good for the country, particularly as an educational device."

Today, the Vietnam Veterans Memorial Fund works to preserve the legacy of the Vietnam Veterans Memorial, to promote healing and to educate about the impact of the Vietnam War. It accomplishes these goals by hosting ceremonies at The Wall; providing free educational materials to middle and high schools; sponsoring a traveling replica of The Wall; and operating a humanitarian program in Vietnam.

(Above) Memorial Fund Founder and President Jan Scruggs touches the Memorial he helped build.

(Right) Volunteers and family members place roses at The Wall on Father's Day.

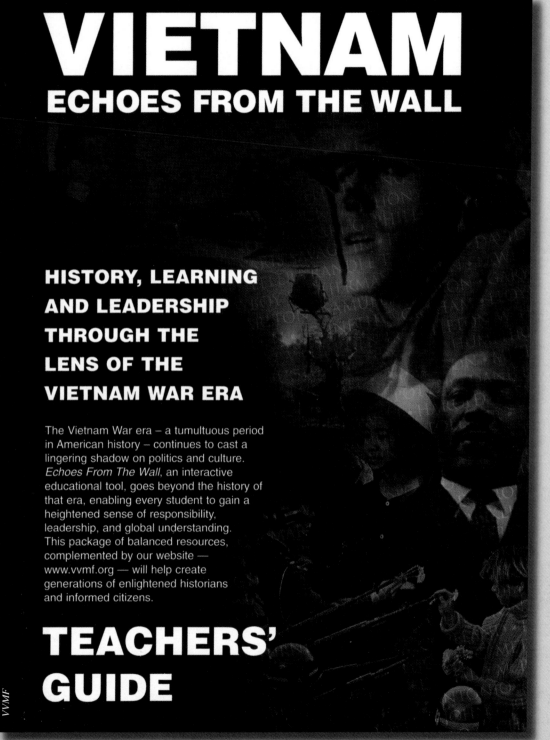

VIETNAM
ECHOES FROM THE WALL

HISTORY, LEARNING AND LEADERSHIP THROUGH THE LENS OF THE VIETNAM WAR ERA

The Vietnam War era – a tumultuous period in American history – continues to cast a lingering shadow on politics and culture. *Echoes From The Wall*, an interactive educational tool, goes beyond the history of that era, enabling every student to gain a heightened sense of responsibility, leadership, and global understanding. This package of balanced resources, complemented by our website — www.vvmf.org — will help create generations of enlightened historians and informed citizens.

TEACHERS' GUIDE

VVMF

The Vietnam Veterans Memorial Fund At a Glance

The Memorial Fund's primary activities include:

• Hosting ceremonies that allow the public to remember and pay tribute to friends and loved ones whose names are inscribed on the Memorial;

• Developing comprehensive and balanced educational materials that incorporate the lessons of the Vietnam War era to provide students with a greater sense of responsibility, leadership and citizenship;

• Recruiting teachers from across the country for membership in the Teach Vietnam Teachers Network, a select group of educators who serve as the Memorial Fund's ambassadors, supporting and promoting its initiatives in their home states;

• Providing educational materials and professional development opportunities for Teachers Network members;

• Coordinating *The Wall That Heals* touring exhibition, featuring a half-scale replica of The Wall and a museum that brings the Memorial's healing legacy to communities across America annually;

• Managing activities and cultivating membership for the Vietnam Veterans Memorial Corporate Council, a distinguished group of leaders in business and government who advance and support the mission of the Memorial Fund;

• Providing the public with an opportunity to learn more about the war, the Memorial and the Memorial Fund through the Web site, *www.vvmf.org*;

• Managing the *In Memory* program that sets aside a day each year to honor those who died as a result of the Vietnam War, but whose deaths do not fit the Department of Defense criteria for inclusion on The Wall;

• Providing nearly 100 Memorial volunteers with the necessary support to continue their useful work of honoring, healing and educating, and hosting an annual appreciation luncheon for these dedicated individuals;

• Commissioning Memorial engineering studies, name additions and status changes;

• Storing extra granite at Quantico Marine Base and purchasing commercial insurance for the Memorial; and

• Providing free name rubbings to the public.

The Vietnam Veterans Memorial Fund is a 501(c)(3) nonprofit organization committed to honoring our nation's veterans and educating this and future generations about the impact of the Vietnam War. Gifts from the public and grants from corporations and foundations provide funding for the Memorial Fund's outreach efforts.

TEACHING ABOUT VIETNAM

An important part of the Memorial Fund's mission is to educate both young and old about the lasting impact of the Vietnam War. Through a variety of educational initiatives, the Memorial Fund provides educators with the necessary tools and resources to teach students about this important era in the nation's history. The Memorial Fund's education programs are supported, in part, by the National Endowment for the Humanities and Time Warner.

The Teach Vietnam programs include: *Echoes From The Wall*; *Echoes From The Mall*; the Teach Vietnam Teachers Network; and *The Legacy of The Wall*.

Echoes From The Wall is a curriculum designed for middle and high school students that provides historical information about the Vietnam War, but also uses the lessons of that chaotic period to imbue future leaders—sitting in classrooms today—with a heightened sense of responsibility, citizenship and service. *Echoes From The Wall* has been distributed free of charge to all 40,000 public and private secondary schools in the country. The package features a teachers' guide, two posters, three books, a video and a war chronology provided by the Veterans of Foreign Wars.

"I've used *Echoes From The Wall* for generating ideas for what I can do in my classroom," explained Chuck Taft, an eighth grade American history teacher in Milwaukee, Wis. Taft uses the *Echoes From The Wall* content and guidelines for state and national curriculum standards, in order to develop lesson plans. In addition, he has developed five lesson plans which focus on Milwaukee-related experiences in Vietnam.

Echoes From The Mall is a field trip guide to help teachers interpret the Vietnam Veterans Memorial for their students. The guide helps to enhance class visits to the Vietnam Veterans Memorial, as well as to the Korean War Veterans Memorial and other points of interest on the National Mall.

A wide variety of suggested on-site and classroom activities offers educators a framework for exploring all elements of the Memorial. The guide contains a variety of activities to use before, during and after a visit. For teachers who are unable to visit Washington, D.C. with their students, the guide also provides a framework for exploring traveling replicas, such as the Memorial Fund's traveling wall, known as *The Wall That Heals*.

Each year, Taft and his eighth grade students travel to Washington, D.C. for a field trip to The Wall. Prior to their visit, "I show them the one name on The Wall that I know of from our school," he explained.

"Then I have them select a name [of a service member on The Wall] from Milwaukee," Taft said. When they visit the Memorial, each student is asked to locate the name on the panels and do a name rubbing. When they return to Milwaukee, students use the Memorial Fund's Web site, *www.vvmf.org*, to conduct research and gather information on their service member. This approach enables Taft to humanize the telling of history for his classes.

Taft is also part of the **Teach Vietnam Teachers Network**, a group of educators throughout the United States who serve as liaisons between the Memorial Fund and their community, state and local school systems. The Teach Vietnam Teachers Network was introduced in 2002 to help broaden The Wall's reach in America's classrooms and to continue the Memorial Fund's important work of educating students about the impact of the Vietnam War. The Memorial Fund provides its Network members with

Members of the Teach Vietnam Teachers Network visit the Three Servicemen statue.

The annual Teachers Conference allows participants to learn from experts and each other.

Leroy Lawson

Tom Estrin

Joe Galloway, (right), co-author of We Were Soldiers Once…And Young, *speaks at the national Teachers Conference.*

Linda Anderson

(Above) Students visit The Wall That Heals traveling memorial at its stop in Elkton, Md.

(At left) A student makes a name rubbing during her visit to The Wall.

free educational materials and professional development opportunities, such as attending regional meetings and the annual national conference. These conferences focus on helping educators learn a variety of ways to teach about the Vietnam War era and enable attendees to share teaching methods and experiences.

Lia Lamb, an eighth grade social studies teacher at Jefferson Junior High School in Woodridge, Ill., is also part of the *Teach Vietnam Teachers Network* and has attended its conferences. "My experience with the Teachers Network has been the most rewarding experience that I've had as a teacher," she explained

The information and networking have given her added resources that she draws on when teaching her Vietnam War unit in class. "It makes that unit better than it ever would have been," she said.

Members of the Teachers Network serve as points of contact for other educators in their states and answer questions about effective teaching of the Vietnam War. They also provide teachers with access to Memorial Fund materials and help educators map the *Echoes From The Wall* curriculum to their state's social studies standards. In addition, Teachers Network members provide feedback about Memorial Fund programs and materials, and help in developing new resources for educators.

The Legacy of The Wall is a traveling storyboard exhibit unveiled by the Memorial Fund in 2000 that is designed to educate viewers, primarily students, about the impact of the Vietnam War.

The exhibit can be displayed at schools and other public facilities. It consists of four interlocking, two-sided panels. On each panel, vivid images, timelines and simple text tell the story of the Vietnam War, The Wall and their lasting legacies. The panels address a range of topics, from the American involvement in Vietnam, life on the home front and the soldiers' experiences to the history of The Wall, Memorial statistics and the different ways we honor our fallen heroes.

The exhibit stands approximately 6 feet tall and runs approximately 15 feet long. An exhibit manual, educational materials and general information about the Memorial Fund accompany the storyboard.

Tom Estrin

People of all ages visit The Wall That Heals.

The Teach Vietnam Teachers Network members leave a wreath at The Wall during the national conference.

VVMF

"The Wall That Heals has become The Wall that educates," said Medal of Honor recipient Brian Thacker during the dedication of the museum trailer.

Vietnam Veterans Memorial The Wall That Heals

THE TRAVELING REPLICA

Millions who have visited the Vietnam Veterans Memorial have experienced its healing power. However, for many, facing The Wall, and the emotions that go with it, is not an easy task. "There are veterans who go down there, but who can't walk to The Wall," explained George "Sandy" Mayo, Vietnam veteran and long-time Memorial Fund board member. "Or [those who] for years…stay away, but, over the course of time, can get down there."

On Veterans Day 1996, as The Wall's healing impact became more evident, the Memorial Fund unveiled a replica of the Vietnam Veterans Memorial, called *The Wall That Heals*, to travel throughout the United States.

Bringing The Wall home to communities throughout the country allows the souls enshrined on the Memorial to exist, once more, among family and friends in the peace and comfort of familiar surroundings. In addition, it enables the many thousands of veterans unable to cope with the prospect of "facing The Wall" to find the strength and courage to do so within their communities, so that their own healing can begin.

The Wall That Heals exhibition features a half-scale replica of the Vietnam Veterans Memorial in Washington, D.C. Like the original Wall, the replica is erected in a chevron shape and is complete with the more than 58,000 names of those killed or missing in action from the conflict. When new names are added to the Memorial in Washington, D.C., *The Wall That Heals* is updated as soon as possible.

As on The Wall in Washington, D.C., the names are listed alphabetically by date of casualty on *The Wall That Heals*. The replica is constructed of powder-coated aluminum, supported by an aluminum frame, and is made up of 24 individual panels, each containing six columns of names. The panels join together to form the nearly 250-foot-wide structure. Each of the replica's two wings is approximately 123 feet long and meets at an angle of 121 degrees, rising to a height of approximately 5 feet at the apex. Each name is laser-etched into the black reflective panels.

A database of names and their precise arrangement on The Wall had to be created to manufacture the panels. The database was then linked to a computer-operated laser system developed solely for the purpose of inscribing *The Wall That Heals*.

The Wall That Heals is transported from community to community by a semi truck and trailer that converts to a museum. Once *The Wall That Heals* is unloaded, the exterior sides of the trailer open to reveal information cases with mementoes left at The Wall and displays that tell the story of the Vietnam War, The Wall and the era surrounding the conflict.

A canvas tent serves as an Information Center, where visitors can find names, either in the *Directory of Names* or by asking one of the volunteers working the computers. Volunteers also have hand-held computer devices, called iPads, that were donated by Fujitsu Transaction Solutions Inc. to help visitors locate names on The Wall more quickly. These iPads are the same ones used by volunteers at The Wall in Washington, D.C.

Entries in the printed directory are in alphabetical order, making it easy to locate a specific name. Each entry is followed by a panel and line number to show where the name can be found on The Wall. Since its dedication, *The Wall That Heals* has visited nearly 250 cities and towns throughout the nation, spreading the Memorial's healing legacy to millions. In addition to its U.S. tour stops, the exhibition has traveled outside of the country to Ireland and Canada.

National sponsors for *The Wall That Heals* include the Disabled American Veterans (DAV) Charitable Trust, Federal Express, Fujitsu Transaction Solutions Inc., Harley-Davidson Foundation and Target Corporation.

Including *The Wall That Heals*, there are five traveling replicas. Most are half-scale; one is three-quarters scale. They are sponsored by private citizens and independent organizations. Collectively, the exhibits strive to meet the demand from communities across the country.

Linda Anderson

(Above) The Wall That Heals has visited over 250 communities. (Right) A museum and information center accompany The Wall That Heals.

VVMF

VA Secretary Jesse Brown, President Bill Clinton and Gen. Colin Powell, USA, Memorial Day 1993.

Sen. John Kerry, Veterans Day 2003.

Gen. Barry R. McCaffrey, USA. Behind him are VA Secretary Jesse Brown and President Bill Clinton.

Jan Scruggs and Bob Hope, Veterans Day 1987.

Wynonna and Naomi Judd, Veterans Day 1987.

Leontyne Price, Veterans Day 1985.

CEREMONIES TO REMEMBER

The Memorial Fund holds six ceremonies at the Vietnam Veterans Memorial each year to help carry out its mission.

Memorial Day and Veterans Day

Every year on Memorial Day and Veterans Day, thousands of veterans and their families congregate at The Wall to remember and to honor those who served in the U.S. armed forces. On these special days, prominent Americans from all walks of life come to the Memorial to deliver thoughtful and patriotic speeches. At the conclusion of these ceremonies, various veterans groups lay wreaths at the Vietnam Veterans Memorial.

Past participants include: Presidents Ronald Reagan and Bill Clinton; Gen. Colin Powell, USA (Ret.), and Gen. Richard Myers, USAF (Ret.); Senators Chuck Hagel (R-Neb.) and John Kerry (D-Mass.); comedian Bob Hope; newscaster Ted Koppel; Miss America 2000 Heather Renee French; and many others. Every president since Reagan has visited the Vietnam Veterans Memorial.

Among those who have lent their musical abilities to the ceremonies are Alabama, Emmy Lou Harris, Graham Nash, Lee Greenwood, Scott McKenzie, Irish tenor John McDermott, the Mormon Choir of Washington and Country Joe MacDonald. These ceremonies are open to all to attend and pay tribute to those who keep our country free.

Families honor loved ones at the In Memory Ceremony 2007.

The Vietnam Veterans Memorial was built to honor all who served and sacrificed in Vietnam, and its black granite walls contain the names of those who gave their lives or remain missing. As years went by, it became clear there was another group that needed to be honored: those who died as a result of the Vietnam War, but whose deaths do not fit the Department of Defense criteria for inclusion on The Wall.

In Memory Day honors these people every year, on the third Monday in April. The first *In Memory* Day ceremony was held in 1999.

During the *In Memory* Day ceremony, the names of all the honorees are read aloud. Family members of the newest inductees are invited to read the names of their loved ones. At the conclusion of the ceremony, individual certificates bearing the name of each honoree, as well as a photo and other information, are placed at the Vietnam Veterans Memorial. The tributes are collected by the National Park

In Memory Day

Service and become part of the Vietnam Veterans Memorial Collection. In addition, the honorees are included in an *In Memory* Honor Roll book to serve as a lasting reminder of their service and sacrifice.

In 2004, a plaque paying tribute to those who served and died prematurely because of their service in Vietnam was added to the Vietnam Veterans Memorial site, near the Three Servicemen statue. This plaque provides families with a special place to remember their loved ones. "I've been to my father's grave once. I don't feel like he's there," explained Dr. Donna Jackson, whose father, Robert G. Gerling, died Jan. 14, 1982 of complications stemming from Agent Orange exposure.

"When there isn't a name to touch, or a rubbing to be had, the plaque is a place where you belong and where people understand your unique circumstance," she added. "It's important having this place where I feel connected, where I can connect with him."

VVMF

Barclay Poling

Crowds come to The Wall in snow and sunshine.

Bill Petros

Barclay Poling

Veterans Day brings many visitors to The Wall. (Above) Sgt.
1st Class Christopher Roussey, U.S. Army Band, plays taps.

At the yearly In Memory Ceremony, loved ones can honor those they lost.

Daniel Arant

Mother's Day at The Wall

Throughout the 1960s and 1970s, countless American mothers watched as their sons and daughters marched off to war in a foreign land. Thousands of these women lost their children to the Vietnam War. And while the pain of that loss is always with them, Mother's Day is a particularly difficult time.

The *Mother's Day at The Wall* ceremony honors their sacrifices while also remembering those who have given their lives for our nation's defense. Each year, American schoolchildren make Mother's Day cards to be read by members of the American Gold Star Mothers and American War Mothers at The Wall on Mother's Day. After reading the cards, the mothers are escorted to The Wall by local Girl Scouts and lay the cards at its base.

American Gold Star Mothers and American War Mothers participate in the Mother's Day Ceremony 2001.

A mother lays a rose at The Wall. (Above) A group of American Gold Star Mothers leaves a wreath at The Wall.

A snowstorm on Veterans Day 1987 did not stop ceremony participants from laying wreaths (top left) and it did not stop the singing group Alabama (above) from performing. (Top right) During a later ceremony, journalist Joe Galloway and Gen. Hal Moore, USA (Ret.), lay a wreath for the 1st Cavalry Division.

Daniel Arant

American Gold Star Mothers and American War Mothers
are given roses during the annual Mother's Day ceremony.

Father's Day Rose Remembrance

Every year for Father's Day, volunteers join sons and daughters of those whose names are inscribed on The Wall to affix 1,000 long-stemmed roses with messages of love and honor sent from across the country to those lost in the war.

Red roses represent those killed in action in Vietnam; yellow roses are for those who remain missing; white is for service members who died in America's most recent war. At the conclusion of the ceremony, participants read some of the thousands of personal messages sent to the Memorial Fund from across the United States. When a specific service member is named in a message, the rose is touched to that person's name on The Wall before being placed at its base, forming a solemn garden of honor and remembrance.

Over 1,000 roses are left at The Wall on Father's Day.

VVMF

Christmas Tree at The Wall

A few days before Christmas each year, the Memorial Fund staff and volunteers decorate a tree at the apex of The Wall. The tree is adorned with thousands of holiday messages sent to the Memorial Fund to honor those who served with the U.S. armed forces in Vietnam and those who are still serving in other military conflicts and their families.

Dave Scavone

Donna Prince

Dave Scavone

Volunteers and members of the public decorate a Christmas tree at The Wall each year.

The tree is decorated with messages sent from across the country.

Leroy Lawson

Daniel Arant

1959

Rajni Sood/VVMF

The Wall is peaceful on a snowy day.

BOM MIN!! NGUY HIỂM!!

DANGER!! MINES!!

William Shugarts

The Memorial Fund's humanitarian program, Project RENEW™, helps children recognize the warning signs for unexploded ordnance and funds the activities of crews that remove the ordnance. (Above right) Ground is broken for a library in the Dakrong District, another Project RENEW™ initiative.

PROJECT RENEW™

William Shugarts

VVMF

In the decades since The Wall was built, the Memorial Fund has created many programs to bring its healing message to Americans. As time went on, opportunities arose that allowed the Memorial Fund to take its message of healing and pursue humanitarian programs overseas—specifically in Vietnam.

In 1999, during a meeting of the Vietnam Veterans Memorial Fund Corporate Council (a group of prominent legislators and corporate leaders who advise the Memorial Fund and share their expertise with its many programs), discussions turned to the upcoming anniversary of the 1975 end of the Vietnam War. Members of the Corporate Council talked about going to Vietnam together as a group. In April 2000, the Memorial Fund led a historic delegation to Vietnam to mark the 25th anniversary of the end of the war.

During that trip, the delegates discovered a tragic truth. An estimated 350,000 tons of land mines and unexploded ordnance (UXO) remain scattered throughout Vietnam from the war, endangering the Vietnamese people.

"We went to Vietnam, saw some of the kids who had their arms, legs and eyes blown out," recalled Scruggs. The delegates realized immediately that something needed to be done.

"We decided this was important for us to do morally and otherwise," Scruggs said.

Out of that realization came Project RENEW™: **R**estoring the **E**nvironment and **N**eutralizing the **E**ffects of **W**ar.

Project RENEW™, the Memorial Fund's humanitarian program, is designed to reduce the threat of land mines and unexploded ordnance in Quang Tri Province, Vietnam. It is a cooperative effort between the Memorial Fund and the Quang Tri Province People's Committee.

Initiated in December 2000, the project focuses on mine awareness education and victim's assistance. During the Vietnam War, Quang Tri Province was divided by the Demilitarized Zone and, as a result, was the most heavily bombed and shelled area of Vietnam.

Several significant steps have been taken to help the Vietnamese people. Quang Tri Television airs public service announcements showing the dangers of land mines and UXO during nightly newscasts, children's programming and other key times. As of fall 2006, there have been 122 television broadcasts and 178 radio broadcasts on mine risk education, plus 38 mine risk education billboards on display.

"Many of the public service announcements are aimed at the kids who were playing with UXO. They had to be told, 'Don't touch it' and be warned of the dangers," explained Holly Rotondi, vice president of programs for the Memorial Fund.

A partnership with the Youth Union, a well-organized network of Vietnamese young adults who meet regularly for social and civic activities, has worked to influence changing behaviors toward the areas throughout Quang Tri Province known to have land mines and UXO. Through coordination with the Youth Union, Project RENEW™ has organized community camping events, parades, art performances and painting competitions in several communes, with games and plays used as effective tools to highlight mine awareness messages.

Efforts by Project RENEW™ staff also have involved working with local health care stations, upgrading the medical systems by providing first aid medical equipment and supplies, and training local health care workers in first aid skills to enhance successful outcomes for victims of land mines and UXO. As of the fall 2006, 485 health care workers have been trained in first aid; 44 medical kits have been provided to communities, health care centers, and regional clinics; and 321 individuals have been beneficiaries of prosthetic and orthotic support.

To assist victims and their families, Project RENEW™ has launched mushroom growing and livestock raising projects, through which many families now have sustainable employment and incomes.

"We're the sponsoring organization, but the Vietnamese are doing it themselves," said Rotondi. "We help them get the funding, but they do the work, and they do a really good job working with their fellow citizens. And they're so proud of it."

"Project RENEW™ has done a lot of good and is making us friends for our country," said Scruggs. "I think the Vietnam Veterans Memorial is the first monument to save people's lives."

(Top) Project RENEW™ has an established presence in Vietnam.

(Middle) Project RENEW™ representative Chuck Searcy (left) stands outside of the office in Dong Ha, Quang Tri Province, Vietnam.

(Bottom) Memorial Fund Founder and President Jan Scruggs points to a shell half-buried in the soil during a visit to Vietnam.

Holly Rotondi

Major League pitcher Danny Graves talks with Vietnamese students.

Danny Graves teaches a Vietnamese girl how to pitch

FROM BATTLEFIELDS TO BALLFIELDS

In 2006, the Memorial Fund and Major League Baseball (MLB) joined together to bring America's favorite pastime to Vietnam. MLB's first Vietnamese-born player, pitcher Danny Graves, agreed to co-host the 2006 "Bringing Baseball to Vietnam" delegation.

Graves was born in Saigon to an American serviceman and a Vietnamese woman who was working at the U.S. Embassy. The Graves family moved to the United States shortly before the fall of Saigon, when Danny was just 14 months old. The delegation was his first trip back. He was accompanied by his mother Thao, who also had not been back in more than 30 years.

During the visit, the delegation presented an exhibition at the National University for Sports and Physical Culture (NUSPC) in Tu Son, near Hanoi. After the presentations, Graves took batting practice and hit a dozen home runs to the delight of the crowd. He also pitched to some of the Vietnamese student athletes.

"It's the most fun I've had in a long time with baseball," Graves said.

The delegation then traveled to Dong Ha Town, Quang Tri Province, to open the country's first-ever baseball field. To ready the site for the field, an Emergency Ordnance Disposal (EOD) team had cleared the area of one artillery shell, two mortars and 11 other types of unexploded ordnance (UXO) in order to make the field safe for play. During the opening ceremony, Scruggs commented, "Here is the opportunity for us to really turn a battlefield into a field of dreams."

While in Vietnam, the Project RENEW™ staff drove home the point that plenty of work remains to be done so that more Vietnamese children can experience the joys of playing baseball in a safe, secure environment. MLB also pledged to continue to work with the Vietnamese people. Since the 2006 delegation, both MLB and the Memorial Fund have been back to nurture the growth and love of baseball in Vietnam and to continue helping the Vietnamese people.

THE MEMORIAL CENTER

For 25 years, the Vietnam Veterans Memorial has resonated with those who lost loved ones, those who lived through the Vietnam era and those who have some special connection to it. The silent but eloquent message of the names on the polished black granite reminds us of the consequences of all wars and the universal themes of service, patriotism and sacrifice.

But to the younger generations who are a growing percentage of the roughly 4 million annual visitors to the Memorial, The Wall experience lacks personal context. To many, it's a brief stop in their class trip to the nation's capital. Yet the very nature of the Memorial and its design prompts a host of questions.

To answer those questions, the Memorial Fund began working in the summer of 2000 to develop a visitor center that could enhance the Memorial experience for current and future generations by teaching about the Vietnam War, its national significance and the impact of The Wall itself on American culture.

"This idea had been bantered about by different people for many years, even the volunteers," explained Scruggs. "Everyone thought, 'Wouldn't it be nice if there was a place where people could go, see photos and learn a bit about the war?'" In essence, an area that would explain what is being memorialized.

Sen. Chuck Hagel (R-Neb.) agreed to sponsor the legislation to create an education center. Endorsements for the idea were obtained from prominent Americans such as Gen. Colin L. Powell, USA (Ret.); former Sen. Bob Dole (R-Kan.), former Presidents Bush and Ford, and respected educators. Groups such as the Veterans of Foreign Wars and the Disabled American Veterans gave it a "thumbs up." Then-Senators Max Cleland (D-Ga.) and Charles Robb (D-Va.) and then-Congressman David Bonior (D-Mich.) also gave their support.

But just as with the efforts to build the Memorial, opponents soon emerged and began trying to block the legislation. Again, Scruggs worked with his allies in Congress to over-

come the hurdles and forge a compromise. It took three years for them to prevail. In November 2003, legislation was signed allowing construction of a Memorial Center underground near the Vietnam Veterans Memorial.

Soon after, the Memorial Fund launched a national design competition, attracting entries from 39 teams of America's best architects, exhibition and landscape designers and engineers. After narrowing the field, the selection committee, with Maya Lin as special advisor, chose the internationally recognized team of Polshek Partnership LLP, architects, and Ralph Appelbaum Associates Inc., exhibit designers, who have created award-winning buildings and inspiring spaces worldwide.

Early on, the Memorial Fund also formed an advisory board of veterans, educators, historians and war journalists, chaired by Gen. Barry R. McCaffrey, USA (Ret.), to explore themes for the Center and serve as a resource for the exhibit designers.

Interested parties testify during a congressional hearing about the Memorial Center held on the National Mall. From left: Jan Scruggs, Vietnam Veterans Memorial Fund; Dorothy Oxendine, American Gold Star Mothers; Rick Jones, AMVETS; and Dennis Cullinan, Veterans of Foreign Wars.

These renderings by Ralph Appelbaum Associates depict various displays planned for the Memorial Center, which will help visitors put faces with the names on The Wall and learn more about these lives that remain unfulfilled.

To raise the funds to build the Memorial Center, an estimated $75 million to $100 million, the Memorial Fund launched a national fundraising effort, chaired by Dr. Christos M. Cotsakos, founder, chairman and CEO of Mainstream Holdings, with Gen. Powell as honorary chair.

The Vietnam Veterans Memorial Center will be a place that touches the heart and teaches the mind, taking people of all ages and walks of life on a journey through the layers of storytelling and history.

"What the Memorial Center will do is to ensure that those names don't just become engravings on a marble wall," explained Powell. "There will come a time when people will not be coming to The Wall to take rubbings, 50 or 100 years from now, maybe even sooner. There will come a time when great-grandchildren will not have the same connection to the names on The Wall, so we want to make sure those names represent a continuing experience. We want to show who these people were, how they lived, what they lived for, what they died for and who they left behind."

The Memorial Center is designed to be inspirational, educational and uplifting, a place for healing and reflection. On entering the Center, visitors will encounter large-scale photos of some of the individuals who made the ultimate sacrifice in Vietnam, bringing the names on The Wall to life and provide an unfiltered glimpse into the realities of war. Their faces will appear on their birthdays, giving friends and relatives a special time to visit and see their loved ones honored at the Center.

Kelly Coleman Rihn, whose father Joel D. Coleman is on The Wall, said, "I like the fact that they're going to show pic-tures on their birthday, to celebrate their life. That also gives me an excuse to go down and visit in March."

Across from the wall of faces will be dramatic glass display cases containing some of the more than 100,000 poems, photos, religious icons, toys, letters and personal effects placed at The Wall. These remembrances speak about the universal bonds of love, friendship and brotherhood that bind veterans together. Visitors will experience their powerful messages as they walk around and through the displays.

"What other memorial is so alive that people come to leave things, hundreds of thousands of things, and everything from graduation cap tassels to motorcycles?" Powell asked.

"And that doesn't even begin to touch the number of times that a name has been rubbed off The Wall and taken home to be framed and hung in a house," he added. "The Wall is alive with the way in which it has touched us all. That's why it's important that we build upon that experience with the education center."

Other exhibits will include a timeline of military events during the war and the story of The Wall itself.

There will also be rotating exhibits and a Resource Center, giving visitors a place to learn about the war and find more in-depth information. "Here's an opportunity to provide an education for young people that they can't get in school and can't get in a movie," said Scruggs.

Ultimately, the Memorial Center will spark visitors to connect those who served in Vietnam to the larger story told on the National Mall. On leaving the Center, visitors will encounter an eloquent sequence of images and quotes from those who served in different wars in different times, reminding them of the human face of war.

VIETNAM VETERANS MEMORIAL FUND

Frances Whitebird of the Sioux Nation blesses the site for the Memorial Center on the 25th anniversary of the groundbreaking for the Vietnam Veterans Memorial.

VVMF

VIETNAM VETERANS MEMORIAL FUND

Your Class Can Help
PUT A FACE
WITH A NAME

LCPL PETER A. PENFOLD
United States Marine Corps
March 17, 1947 – October 17, 1967
Panel 28 E, Line 29
Photo courtesy of his mother,
Jeanne Penfold

A Project to Teach
Students about
the Lessons of War

Sponsored by the Veterans of Foreign Wars of the U.S.

THE MEMORIAL FUND WEB SITE:
WWW.VVMF.ORG

The Memorial Fund's Web site, *www.vvmf.org*, has a host of information about the group's mission, programs and ceremonies, as well as historical facts about the Vietnam Veterans Memorial.

Once on the site, visitors can go to "The Virtual Wall" and look up names that are on the Vietnam Veterans Memorial. Profiles for each name give information about the service member, as well as a place for friends and loved ones to post digital remembrances and photos.

The Memorial Fund's Virtual Wall was launched on Nov. 10, 1998 during a White House ceremony hosted by Vietnam veteran and then-Vice President Al Gore.

Today, the Memorial Fund's Virtual Wall features nearly 200,000 messages, anecdotes and photographs and provides visitors with the ability to view digital name rubbings similar to those that can be made at The Wall in Washington, D.C.

PUT A FACE WITH A NAME

The success of the Memorial Fund's Virtual Wall and all of the photos posted there made a thought gradually emerge: wouldn't it be wonderful to have photos for all of the service members whose names are on The Wall? With the creation of the Wall of Faces in the Vietnam Veterans Memorial Center, this idea becomes even more urgent.

The *Put a Face with a Name* campaign started in September 2001 as a joint effort between the Memorial Fund and Kinko's Inc. to collect a picture for each of the more than 58,000 men and women whose names are inscribed on The Wall.

More than 2,500 photo remembrances were added to The Virtual Wall during the four-month program. While Kinko's involvement ended in December of that year, the momentum gained through that joint effort continued. Today, the site features nearly 10,000 images of those who gave the ultimate sacrifice or who remain missing. *(If you have a photo of a loved one whose name is on The Wall that you would like to contribute, see Appendix 4 for details.)*

(Previous page) Schoolchildren make a name rubbing.

(Inset, previous page) A mother and daughter pause to read a Father's Day card.

(This page, right) Roses are placed along The Wall on Father's Day.

VVMF

Rajni Sood/VVMF

Nearly 25 years later, visitors are still leaving remembrances honoring those who were lost during the Vietnam War.

Visitors of all ages gather at The Wall for Memorial Day 2007.

WALL MAGIC

PIECES OF THE WALL
BY
NANCY SMOYER

- A man stands by a panel where he has placed a large picture frame containing pieces of a boy's life: a picture of the young man in uniform, a newspaper article about him as a football star and one about his death, the letter from his commanding officer to the family. A couple comes up to look at it, and the man says to his wife, "I knew that man. I served with him." The other man hears him and says, "That's my brother."

- A young man with short hair and a fit body asks to do nine rubbings of one name on the last panel. It's his father who was in Special Forces, and he too is a Green Beret and will be going to the Persian Gulf in a month.

- A woman stands in front of her brother's panel. A man nearby asks a volunteer for six rubbing papers. The woman knows that when her brother was killed, 18 others in his platoon also died, so she asks the man if he was a Marine and if he's looking at the same day. He says yes, he was in the same company, but he doesn't know her brother or the man who died trying to save him. But he has buddies who are on The Wall with them and he was in the area at the time, so he is able to tell her what happened that day.

- A vet is at the information booth trying to locate his buddy's name on the directory computer. He knows the name should be there because he put him onto a chopper, badly wounded, but the name can't be found. While they are searching, another man comes up looking for his buddy's name, which he, too, can't find. He had seen his platoon take devastating mortar fire at the LZ as he was being medevaced out. And then the two men realize that they are looking for each other.

- A group of Soviet veterans who fought in Afghanistan come to visit their American comrades with whom they have so much in common in the wars they fought, both in foreign countries and at home. They place a folded flag from their country at the base of The Wall, and standing quietly around it, one by one place a red carnation across the flag. Someone speaks briefly in Russian, and then they slowly disperse. At another time, Soviet Afghan veterans leave a cigarette, a shot glass and a piece of bread: the traditional salute to fallen comrades.

- Two men see another man doing a rubbing of the same person they are there to visit. When they talk, they find that the man doing the rubbing was his best friend in high school, and the other two were his buddies in Vietnam. The vets say that they would like to get a message to his family, that there are people who still care. They tell the childhood friend that they have both named their first child after their buddy: both girls, both named Chris. The vets ask if the friend would like to know more about how Chris died, and they go off together talking.

The majesty and serenity of The Wall is enhanced by a recent snowfall.

Nancy Smoyer is a volunteer at The Wall. She lives in Fairbanks, Alaska.

Rajni Sood/VVMF

The Washington Monument is reflected on the granite panels of The Wall.

The east wall and Washington Monument
are outlined by the sunrise.

Clouds are reflected on The Wall as migrating
birds pass the Washington Monument.

A veteran makes several name rubbings during a visit to The Wall.

Daniel Arant

CHAPTER 5

VOLUNTEERS

Leroy Lawson

Sara McVicker

VVMF

Daniel Arant

(Above) A volunteer kneels by The Wall.

(Top left) Two veterans embrace by The Wall, May 1984.

(Top right) Volunteer Emmelene Gura helps a veteran find a name.

VOLUNTEERS

In 1982, during construction of The Wall, many feared vandals might try to deface or destroy the panels. "People had threatened to come at night and bulldoze it over," recalled James "J.C." Cummings, the current architect of record for the Vietnam Veterans Memorial. In response, a handful of veterans began to stand guard at the site. "They were there to literally protect the Memorial," he said.

Even after the dedication ceremonies, the veterans continued to stand vigil. That is when it was discovered that visitors were coming to The Wall in the middle of the night, despite the fact that there were no lights. To help these late-night visitors see better, the veterans began to bring handheld lanterns so they could escort people and help them find names. These were the first volunteers at The Wall.

Since then, volunteers have become an integral part of the Memorial experience for millions of annual visitors.

A HUG AT THE WALL

On a daily basis, volunteers provide answers to commonly asked questions about the Memorial. They help visitors locate names, using both the *Directory of Names* located at either side of the Memorial and the handheld iPad computers donated by Fujistu. They make name rubbings and offer comfort to those who may be overcome with emotion. "Essentially, the volunteers at the Memorial breathe life into the experience for so many of the tourists and the veterans," said Jan Scruggs, Memorial Fund founder and president.

"Volunteers are there every day of the year. They are there when no one else is," he continued. "Oftentimes, there will be one or two park rangers in charge of the Korean, Vietnam and Lincoln Memorials. People don't usually need someone to talk to at the Korean and Lincoln Memorials; whereas at the Vietnam Veterans Memorial, sometimes people want to talk with someone.

"People have more questions there because they're drawn into a social interaction with the Memorial and with the people around them," he added.

"Veterans who come to The Wall sometimes come by themselves, sometimes with other people," explained volunteer and Vietnam veteran Charlie Harootunian. "I can usually tell if they're a veteran by the way they're at The Wall. At first, I'll try to be unobtrusive. Then I'll approach and ask, 'Is there anything I can do for you? Do you want me to look up a name for you or do you want to talk?' Some guys will say they don't want to talk, but then the next thing you know we're sitting on a bench having a conversation."

When he began volunteering, Harootunian had the most difficult time talking with the parents, the widows and the children of those on The Wall. "It was very difficult to deal with; it just tore my heart apart," he recalled. "I try to keep myself composed. It's not as hard as it used to be. At times, I have to take a walk after I speak with someone. But it's not about me; it's about helping them."

Once, while Harootunian was working at The Wall, three couples approached him and asked for help in finding a name. One of the women in the group broke down and began to cry. She was the mother of the man whose name they were searching for. Quietly, the group explained to Harootunian that they had traveled from Florida and that it was the only trip they were going to be able to make to see the Memorial. The group walked slowly to one of the benches and sat down.

"I felt there was something I had to say to her," recalled Harootunian. "I let them compose themselves, then I went up to her and said, 'I know this is your first time here, but I want you to know that your son has not been forgotten by those who served. Veterans by the thousands come here to remember. It's important for you to know and to understand that they think of him every day.'"

Long-time volunteer Annmarie Emmet said, "I've had more volunteers ask about how to handle the situation when someone is having a hard time. There's nothing like a touch or a hug that can't get somebody past something. Every volunteer down there is a good hugger, male or female. And I see no hesitation on the [part of the] vets to hug."

Reassuring words can also help. Volunteer Lee Adriani recalled one day when she saw a nurse escorting a blind man who was missing one arm. "The [man] got very upset because he couldn't think of the names of any of the boys [he had served

Daniel Arant

Sometimes support is what is needed most. At right, volunteer Betty Henry hugs a veteran.

In Their Own Words

When asked about their time at The Wall, here are some thoughts from volunteers.

"One year, my daughter participated in the Father's Day Rose Remembrance with me. While reading the tributes, I cried because I realized how fortunate I was to be able to have my daughter with me while those on The Wall were able to be with their loved ones in memory only."

Anthony Fasolo
Leesburg, Va.
Vietnam veteran

Volunteers arrive early to prepare roses for Father's Day.

VVMF

Volunteer Art Drescher gathers American flags and POW/MIA flags to distribute to visitors before a ceremony at The Wall.

with]," said Adriani. "I told him that was very common, because usually they knew the guys by their nicknames."

Volunteers at The Wall are incredibly generous with their time. All volunteers considered "active" by NPS give at least 144 hours or more of their time annually on the National Mall; however the majority of volunteers at The Wall give closer to 500 hours. They spend this time in the heat and the cold, just to be available for the visitor in need.

"I have never been down there—all hours of the day and night, no matter what the weather is—that someone hasn't been down there," said veteran and volunteer Stephen "Red" Flegal. "You'll see footprints in the snow when they haven't shoveled."

"Some [visitors] are more comfortable coming at night," explained Harootunian. "No one can see them, and they can't see anyone." Some veterans have difficulty approaching The Wall. Many will venture no closer than the tree line. Others require the gentle assistance and escort of a volunteer who offers encouragement and support with every step.

In addition to their time at The Wall, many volunteers also assist the Memorial Fund with the six ceremonies it holds annually at The Wall, its outreach programs, such as the Teach Vietnam Teachers Network Conference and *The Wall That Heals*, a half-scale traveling replica of The Wall.

The dedication and commitment of these outstanding individuals is honored each year at the Volunteer Appreciation Luncheon hosted by the Memorial Fund. A highlight of the luncheon is the presentation of The Libby Hatch Volunteer Recognition Award, named after long-time Memorial Fund employee Libby Hatch, whose dedication to the Memorial was extraordinary. She died in a motorcycle accident in 1998.

In a speech given during one of the luncheons, Libby's brother Ted Hatch addressed the powerful presence and purpose of the volunteers at The Wall. "As Memorial volunteers, you allow people to slow down time and space and to focus on what the Vietnam War means to them, right at that moment, right when they freely come to embrace their own feelings and thoughts and maybe reconcile them," he said.

"For the pilgrims who come to The Wall, it is as if you sprinkle pixie dust and memorialize the hallowed grounds," he added. "You make the Memorial a living monument, like Gettysburg with a face, offering a strong, yet unobtrusive shoulder to cry on, a living testament to compassion and healing for a people and a nation."

Volunteer Sid George makes a name rubbing.

Volunteer Lee Adriani talks with children at the National Park Service kiosk.

Nancy Smoyer comes from Alaska to volunteer at The Wall.

Frank Bosch was a dedicated volunteer for over 20 years. He was a veteran of WWII, Korea and Vietnam.

Volunteer Paddy Wiesenfeld, Ph.D., helps out at The Wall.

FROM FAR AND WIDE

ost Vietnam Veterans Memorial volunteers are registered with and work for the National Park Service (NPS). NPS volunteers are qualified to serve at any of the memorials in the nation's capital, although there is a core group who devote their time solely at The Wall.

These volunteers hail from as many as 20 different states and the District of Columbia and from as far away as Alaska. Many, like Flegal and Harootunian, have been committed volunteers for 20 years or more. Adriani volunteered for 25.

Emmet has also been volunteering at The Wall for almost 20 years. A native Washingtonian, she lives a short distance from the Memorial. Her brother served in Vietnam and a friend of her older brother has his name on The Wall.

In 1986, she was volunteering at a local hospital and saw a notice advertising the need for NPS volunteers at The Wall. "To me, it was an opportunity to be outside," she recalled. Initially,

she said, "I would come in the evening or afternoons. After I retired in 1999, I did some weekdays and longer hours on the weekends."

Volunteers set their own schedules and hours, dedicating as much or as little time as they can give. Most local volunteers have predictable routines, working on specific days or times of day. "Everyone has settled into a pattern," said Emmet. "There are usually about four or six volunteers during the weekends and one on weekdays. Then on holidays, we have as many as 10 or 20 volunteers, people who have moved away or only come down for a day or who come down for three or four days."

Many volunteers who travel from out of town work the same dates or weekends each year. Flegal, who lives in Pennsylvania, has traveled regularly to volunteer at the Memorial since 1983. "I always come down for the week at Memorial

Day and Veterans Day, as well as for Father's Day and Mother's Day, and holidays like the 4th of July," explained Flegal.

Volunteers who work on the same dates each year often have the opportunity to reconnect with one another. Frequently, they also see returning visitors year after year. "You really get to renew old friendships on holidays," Flegal said. He and several others from out of town often coordinate their trip schedules so they can share hotel rooms and expenses, as well as volunteer and carpool together.

"They're like a family. They may see each other only once or twice a year, but they're bonded," said Holly Rotondi, vice president of programs for the Memorial Fund.

During her time at the Memorial, Emmet has also made several close friends. "You're all there for the same purpose," she explained. "It's different from other friends because we have this one common experience."

Having a meeting at The Wall are (from left) volunteers Lee Adriani, Allen McCabe and Leroy Lawson,
Memorial Fund Vice President of Programs Holly Rotondi and volunteer Suzanne Sigona.

Bill Petros

THE "YELLOW HATTERS"

Through the years, volunteers have worn a variety of different NPS uniforms while on the job. One constant has been their yellow hats, which are responsible for their nickname, the "yellow hatters." For years, Adriani decorated her hat with pins that had been given to her by visitors to The Wall. "They mean a lot to me," she said.

Formal training for volunteers is brief, but new volunteers are usually mentored by the more experienced. "Training can happen two ways," explained Emmet. "You can spend time with a ranger or with another volunteer. They'll take you down to The Wall and give you the highlights. But much of it is on-the-job training.

"Mostly, the Park Service wants us to remember that we represent the NPS and we must act accordingly," she added.

Volunteer Dan Arant is one of The Wall's most prolific photographers. Here, he takes a shot of a keepsake left at The Wall by Ann Pruett, who watches at left. Fellow volunteer Donna Prince also observes.

WHY THEY VOLUNTEER

Often, their reasons for volunteering at The Wall are intensely private and personal. "Many people don't want to say why they give their time," explained Rotondi. "Sometimes, it's because they are veterans themselves and they [feel they] owe it to their buddies on The Wall. Others lived through that era, and it affected them growing up." Rotondi noted that within the last five years, a growing number of Baby Boomer retirees are becoming volunteers, now that they have more free time.

For Harootunian, the notion to volunteer at The Wall came to him in 1986. He was at Arlington National Cemetery attending the burial of his platoon sergeant. After the service, the sergeant's widow asked Harootunian if he and his wife would accompany her to The Wall. She had never visited it before. While there, Harootunian recalled, "I saw a volunteer with a cap on and [I] asked about the program. 'What are the requirements?' 'It's whatever you want to do, whenever you want to do it,' [the volunteer replied.] That sounded good to me!" said Harootunian.

For many years, Harootunian, who lives in Massachusetts, had a job that involved travel. He would plan client visits for a Friday morning in Washington, D.C., then volunteer that night and through the weekend before returning home Sunday night. "My wife gave me plenty of room," he said. "She saw a difference in me after the times I was volunteering. At times, she would even look at me and tell me, 'You need to go down and spend some time at The Wall.'"

Kelly Coleman Rihn of Glenshaw, Pa., whose father's name is on The Wall, is one of the youngest volunteers. "Visitors always ask why I do this," she said. "My dad's name is on this Wall. We're here to keep the memory alive. I've been helped by so many veterans and others, I want to give back."

She has also grown particularly close with several other volunteers, all of whom are veterans. "They're like uncles to me," she added. "I look at them as a gift my dad gave me. If I didn't go down there [to The Wall], I wouldn't have met these guys."

NAME RUBBINGS

In November 1982, as the dedication ceremonies for The Wall came to a close, the crowds pressed forward to get closer, to touch the Memorial, to see the names. That afternoon, although no one remembers the exact specifics of how or when, a ritual was sparked. It involved holding a piece of paper flat against a panel and rubbing a pencil's edge across each letter beneath it in order to create a shadowed stencil of a name from The Wall, much like gravestone or relief rubbings are done. The practice of making name rubbings at The Wall had begun.

Name rubbings hold special meaning for visitors, allowing them to take away a unique and immensely personal memento. Colleen Pontes, whose father Kevin Joyce was added to The Wall in 2003, remembered, "I did a name rubbing that day. Then I did several more and gave them away for Christmas that year."

At first, many visitors used the Memorial's small fact sheet as rubbing paper. "It was a green information brochure that people started doing rubbings on," recalled Flegal. Today, the NPS kiosk stocks supplies for name rubbings. Volunteers carry special artist pencils and paper slips created especially for name rubbings.

One side of the paper features *The Vietnam Veterans Memorial* in large bold type; the bottom portion of the sheet is blank, leaving a space for a rubbing. Information provided on the reverse side enables visitors to locate service dates on The Wall which can be helpful when a visitor does not have a specific name.

Volunteers Paul and Cyndy Stancliff's embrace is reflected on The Wall.

Leroy Lawson

In Their Own Words

"Making a rubbing of an individual name for a loved one and listening to the story associated with the name symbolizes the impact of war...What do you say to a mother who asks you to do a rubbing of the names of her two sons?"

Dan Arant
Annapolis, Md.
Vietnam veteran

Rubbings provide a remembrance for the people who visit The Wall.

Initially, in the months following the dedication, people were allowed to go on top of The Wall to try to reach the names from above. "I went with one woman up on the top. She leaned over and got to touch the name," Adriani recalled. In addition, visitors often placed candles at the top of The Wall. Unfortunately, as the candles burned, wax melted down the face of the panels. NPS put a stop to these practices in order to protect both visitors and the Memorial.

Instead, NPS equipped volunteers with ladders so that they could reach the highest names on the panels. Two ladders are kept at the Memorial for this purpose. "As long as it's not too high up, the visitors can do the rubbing," explained Adriani. "If they cannot reach it, it has to be done by a volunteer or ranger." Visitors are not allowed to use the ladders.

Thousands of Americans who are unable to visit The Wall receive free name rubbings from the Memorial Fund each year. Every week, volunteers bring paper and pencil to The Wall to continue the work that keeps alive the memory of an American hero who gave his or her life decades ago. *(See Appendix 4 for more information.)*

Another option for those who live far away from the Memorial is to view a "virtual" name rubbing. On the Memorial Fund's Web site, there is a section called "The Virtual Wall" that allows visitors to look up a person whose name is on The Wall, read some information about that person's service and leave a remembrance. Once a visitor is in a specific person's profile, he or she can click on a button to bring up a digital name rubbing.

IN THEIR OWN WORDS

"As a Vietnam survivor, I hold a deep sense of obligation to those whose names are listed. When I volunteer, I act as THEIR spokesman to convey to visitors how significant their sacrifice was."

Ron Edgington
Lincoln University, Pa.
Vietnam veteran

Dave Scavone

Volunteer Ron Edgington brings the Christmas tree to The Wall each year. Here, he helps decorate it with messages of tribute.

IN THEIR OWN WORDS

*"I really think it is the total ex-
perience, not just one, that has made
it easier for me to go down those
walkways with all the names looking
at you without that nagging question,
'Why them and not me?'"*

Michael Coale
Forked River, N.J.
Vietnam veteran

1959

Volunteer Mike Coale helps decorate the Christmas tree at The Wall.

The "Can Do" Squad

Because the Memorial Fund hosts a variety of special ceremonies at The Wall each year, NPS volunteers also assist with many of the event planning tasks. "In the beginning, we were looking up names and answering questions. There was no real formal structure," explained Flegal. "We would help out during services and ceremonies. Then it got more formalized with the 10th anniversary [of The Wall]." At that point, volunteers became more heavily involved in the ceremony preparation and setup. They are also instrumental in escorting visitors to their seats during events and in assisting with crowds.

One core group of long-time volunteers that helps the Memorial Fund has been nicknamed the "Can Do" Squad. The initial group of four veterans includes Michael Coale, Red Flegal, Charlie Harootunian and Ron Worstell. One honorary member, Rick Barrett, has joined the group in recent years.

"The 'Can Do' Squad can do everything," explained Rotondi. "They do the heavy work preparing for Memorial Day and Veterans Day. They run around at midnight, trucking and carrying and lugging boxes for me. I leave them in charge and don't have to worry about things getting done."

In 2004, the "Can Do" Squad returned to Vietnam together during a Memorial Fund delegation. All veterans, this was the first time any of them had been back since they served.

A Special Bond

A special bond has developed between volunteers, particularly the veterans and the American Gold Star Mothers, as well as with the children of those who died, many of whom belong to the organization Sons and Daughters in Touch.

"Volunteering has given me the opportunity to get to know the Gold Star Moms very well," Flegal said. "Seeing how strong they are and their commitment to all veterans, despite having lost their own child, has greatly affected my life."

"They have such a connection. There's an allegiance," Rotondi said. Many feel it is their duty to take care of the moms, daughters and sons of their buddies, she explained.

Other volunteers echoed similar thoughts. "It's important for us to be involved with the sons and daughters," explained Harootunian. "There's still a lot who need to be cared for. Loss doesn't necessarily get better with time."

(Top) Volunteers meet at The Wall in November 2004: Rick Barrett, Stephen "Red" Flegal, Sid George, Ron Edgington and Michael Coale.

(Bottom) The "Can-Do" Squad and Memorial Fund dignitaries congratulate Charlie Harootunian after he receives the Volunteer of the Year Award in 2003. From left: Rick Barrett, Ron Worstell, Brig. Gen. George Price, Jan Scruggs, Charlie Harootunian, Mike Coale and Red Flegal.

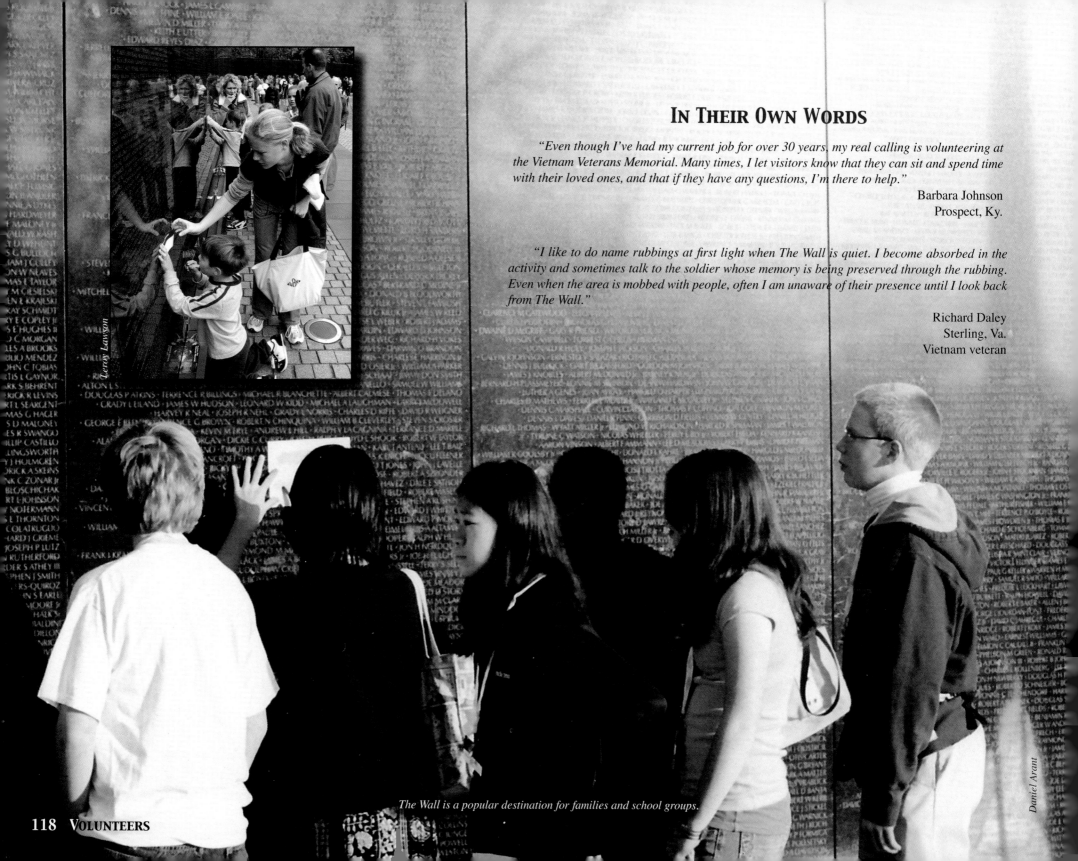

IN THEIR OWN WORDS

"Even though I've had my current job for over 30 years, my real calling is volunteering at the Vietnam Veterans Memorial. Many times, I let visitors know that they can sit and spend time with their loved ones, and that if they have any questions, I'm there to help."

Barbara Johnson
Prospect, Ky.

"I like to do name rubbings at first light when The Wall is quiet. I become absorbed in the activity and sometimes talk to the soldier whose memory is being preserved through the rubbing. Even when the area is mobbed with people, often I am unaware of their presence until I look back from The Wall."

Richard Daley
Sterling, Va.
Vietnam veteran

Leroy Lawson

Daniel Arant

The Wall is a popular destination for families and school groups.

Maintaining Order, Offering Insight

Part of a volunteer's job involves reminding visitors, particularly larger tour and student groups, that the Memorial grounds should be treated appropriately. "If you walk down without a T-shirt, I'll ask you to put it on," said Flegal. "This is a memorial; we want them to act respectfully. Occasionally, runners will run through, and we'll ask them not to."

"Starting with the first of March, you'll get eight to 10 buses of schoolchildren," said Emmet. "If they've got a good school, a good teacher and they're well-prepared, they're respectful. On the other hand, [sometimes] you do have to remind people."

In addition to maintaining order, volunteers serve as docents for The Wall. Frequently, Emmet will notice visitors gazing up at the date on the eastern arm's first panel. "They see the 1959 and that can open up a whole dialog,' she explained. "When you see people looking up and puzzled, it's a great opener for a conversation."

"I enjoy explaining how The Wall is laid out. It isn't just two black granite walls. There's a reason for why it is the way it is. There's a story as to why the black granite was chosen, how the names are laid out," she added. "It's easy to do in a few minutes. You can give them enough information to pique their interest and help them understand."

"I try to stand near the panels where I served, in case someone comes up to see a name of someone who died then," Harootunian said. In this way, he might be able to offer a visitor both comfort and insight regarding events of that time.

Emmet has noticed through the years that the types of visitors and questions have changed. "One of the biggest changes in the last two to three years is in the interest in the number of fatalities," she said. Emmet believes that the current Iraq war has prompted an increased level of awareness regarding the toll of war, particularly among middle-schoolers and young people.

Another change she has witnessed is the greater number of older visitors to The Wall since the completion of the World War II Memorial. Many tours to the WWII Memorial include The Wall on their itinerary. Those visitors, Emmet explained, "are students of the wars. They have a little bit more knowledge and interest in the wars."

The Vietnam Veterans Memorial is one of the most visited memorials in Washington, D.C. For those who can't visit, volunteers like Emmelene Gura (shown above) make name rubbings.

A Day in the Life of a Volunteer at The Wall
BY
Nancy Smoyer

The volunteer is coming on duty. She walks quickly to the National Park Service kiosk to sign in and get the *Directory of Names*, rubbing papers and pamphlets. She puts on her yellow volunteer hat and starts toward The Wall.

Her pace slows as she pauses to acknowledge the statue of the three fighting men with the thousand-yard stare and slows even more as she leaves the hectic pace of the outside world to adapt to the slower, quieter rhythm of The Wall. As she walks the length of The Wall, she scans the visitors looking for anyone who needs assistance. She reads the letters and makes note of other items that have been left by earlier visitors: a high school varsity letter, a newspaper article, a Purple Heart, a picture of a squad of men in Vietnam, many flowers, a POW/MIA bracelet.

And so her day begins.

A family comes down the walkway. The little girl is skipping and laughing. Her mother stoops down to talk to her, telling her that this is a serious place. The names of lots of men and women who died in a war in Vietnam are on that Wall, and their families and friends are coming to see their names. They continue on, the mother holding her daughter's hand as she walks quietly by her side.

A man with graying hair, wearing a business suit, walks slowly down the pathway. His body is tight, his hands by his sides. He looks only down or at The Wall, stopping occasionally. The volunteer watches him go by, knowing he will be back. She hands out a few pamphlets, explains to a couple how the names on The Wall are arranged, and keeps an eye on the man. She looks up the name of a high school classmate for a woman, directs her to the name, offers rubbing paper, and watches the man.

He walks slowly back, and she goes over to him and quietly asks, "How are you doing?"

He says, "OK," stops and quickly turns out toward the grass, fighting for composure.

She waits, then says, "Is this your first time here?"

He says, "Yes." And so a conversation begins.

They talk about the war and the people he knew there: the ones who made it back and those who didn't. She asks how he's been doing since he got back, and he says pretty well, but he has a friend—a buddy of his from Vietnam—who is hurting. She urges him to encourage his friend to go to a vet center and to bring him to The Wall so the healing process can begin.

After talking for a half an hour or so, he prepares to leave.

"I didn't think I wanted to talk to anyone, but I'm glad you stopped me," he says. She gives him a hug.

A group of three men are talking animatedly, exchanging stories, happy to be there together. After a while, the volunteer goes over to them, curious about who they are and what brought them there. She learns that they demonstrated against the war and now counsel veterans. One does outreach service with Vietnam vets who live isolated lives in the woods of New England. As they continue talking, one of the men asks about her connection with The Wall, and she shows them the name of a Marine she knew and tells them the story of his death. The ex-protester rubs his fingers over the name again and again, as tears flow down his face.

A woman walks back and forth along The Wall, crying. The volunteer offers her a tissue, and she stops to talk. She didn't know anyone who died in Vietnam and only a few who went, but the impact of the names has overwhelmed her.

Another veteran comes to The Wall for the first time after years of flying in and out of Washington, D.C. as a pilot. He was also a pilot in Vietnam. When asked why he came on that particular summer day, he answers, "Because it's hot and humid." There it is.

A group of veterans come. Most are wearing parts of their uniforms from Vietnam. They are a vet center group, and they have worked through to this goal of coming together to see their buddies on The Wall. They hug and cry and laugh and tell stories—and go away lighter.

A distinguished-looking couple blends in with the other visitors. They go directly to a panel and a name and stop. She wonders again why no one from his platoon ever got in touch with them. She dabs her eyes. He puts his arm around her. They pause for a few moments, then walk off.

A 12-year-old boy stands crying among his classmates. The girls try to comfort him, while the boys giggle self-consciously. The volunteer goes over, puts her arm around him and asks if he has a relative on The Wall. He shakes his head no, but says his mother's boyfriend's name is there. They go off together to do a name rubbing for his mother.

A young man walks up to the volunteer and shows her his silver POW/MIA bracelet. He says he's been wearing one for the past five years—not the same bracelet, because he gives them away to people who show interest, but each bracelet had the same name. He wants to find that name. The volunteer locates it in the directory and takes him to it. She shows him the plus sign next to the name that indicates the man is missing. She tells him how that sign will be changed to a diamond if the man's remains are found or a circle will be drawn around the plus sign if he returns alive.

A group of women of varying ages slowly filters in. They are nurses. They locate a woman's name on the last panel, and one of the nurses tells the volunteer that the two of them were on the plane that was airlifting orphans out of Saigon when it crashed on take-off. Several of her friends are together on The Wall in the lines for those last few days of the war.

A man comes down with his tour group and asks for help finding a name. The man on The Wall was a neighbor of his family who used to shovel their walk in the winter. The volunteer offers to do a rubbing for him, and as she finishes it, she asks if the soldier's family has been to The Wall. The man says "No," so another rubbing is done for him to take home to them. And then a third rubbing is made to give to his own parents in memory of their neighbor.

A jogger, face glistening, clothes wet, walks by greeting the volunteer with a smile. He pauses briefly at a name and goes on out to continue his run.

A vet in jungle fatigues bedecked with ribbons, medals, patches and pins stands alone in front of a panel with a single red rose. She can tell he's been there before and goes over to talk. He says a buddy of his was blown up over there by a grenade. It's the one death he couldn't get over after the war. But when he came to The Wall a couple of years ago, that settled it for him. He doesn't know why except that seeing his friend's name on The Wall with all the others made it final, resolved. But he won't forget, so he wears a black bracelet with his buddy's name engraved on it.

Finally, it's dark. The volunteer's back is aching. She has a slight sunburn, and she knows her ankles will be swollen that night. She starts to leave, but sees a man coming along alone who might need help. Then his buddy catches up with him, so she starts out again. A couple asks about the dates 1959 and 1975. She explains and gives them a pamphlet. There are only a few people there now. More will come later tonight when they can be alone. She takes off her hat, passes "her" name and goes on out.

Nancy Smoyer is a volunteer at The Wall.
She lives in Fairbanks, Alaska.

WALL MAGIC

"Wall Magic" is a term that was coined for those moments of unexplained coincidences and mysteries that often occur at the Memorial. They are the moments when two strangers are standing side by side searching a panel, only to discover that they are both looking for the same name. They are those times when veterans from the same platoon run into each other on the grounds at the Memorial after decades of not having seen one another. They are the tender times when a nurse realizes during a ceremony at The Wall that she has just met the parents of a man she held while he lay dying.

Wall Magic moments have happened innumerable times. Many of the core volunteers, because they have spent so many years at the Memorial, have several Wall Magic stories to share.

"On two occasions, I've run into people who were neighbors of guys I served with," remembered Harootunian. "One day, these visitors were trying to get a rubbing. The name was high [up on the panel] and they asked for help. When I asked for the name, I couldn't believe it was someone I had served with." Such a coincidence may not sound astounding, except for the fact that around 4 million people visit The Wall each year.

Daniel Arant

Volunteer Nancy Smoyer (above) has witnessed many examples of Wall Magic during her years as a volunteer.

(Right) Many visitors feel compelled to touch The Wall.

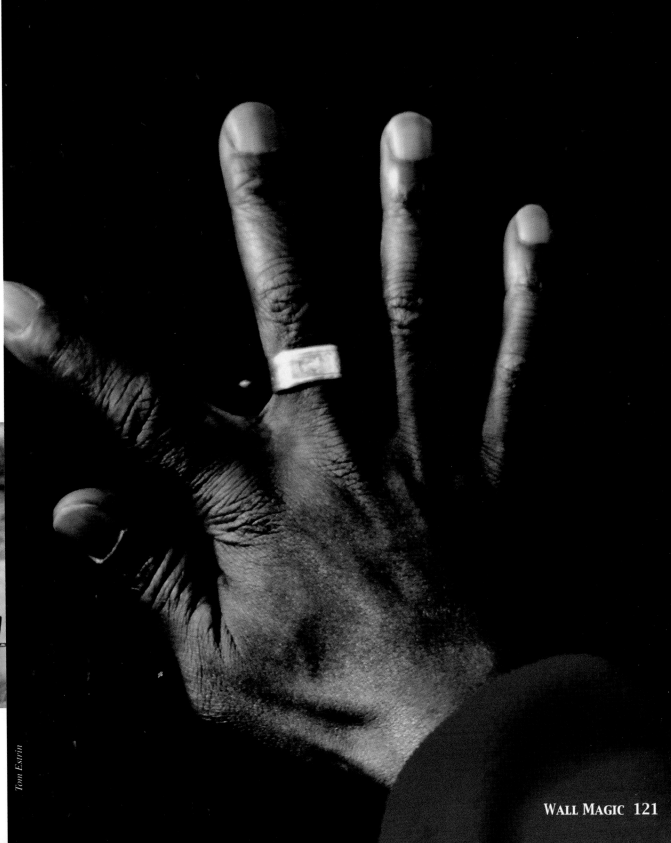

Tom Estrin

Some school groups and other visitors leave wreaths when they visit.

HAMP COOPER
ELEMENTARY SCHOOL

1975

The Three Servicemen statue has been praised for its fine detail.

123

THE LIBBY HATCH SPECIAL RECOGNITION AWARD

Elizabeth Denison Hatch, known as Libby by her family, friends and countless Vietnam veterans, had a passion for life, a fiery exterior and a sentimental heart. In 1991, Libby joined the Vietnam Veterans Memorial Fund and worked closely with its Founder and President Jan Scruggs organizing many events at The Wall, including the annual Memorial and Veterans Day ceremonies, and working closely with the volunteers.

Sadly, on Dec 6, 1998, Hatch was killed in a motorcycle accident.

To honor her memory, the Memorial Fund, with the Hatch family, awards The Libby Hatch Special Recognition Award yearly to the volunteer who most exemplifies the commitment, dedication and passion espoused by Hatch. Recipients of The Libby Hatch Special Recognition Award possess strong convictions, fierce loyalty and a warm heart channeled into honoring our nation's Vietnam veterans and promoting healing among all those affected by the Vietnam War.

The award reflects Libby's unique impact on the volunteers who serve as ambassadors to the Memorial, ensuring that her warm spirit will be passed on to new volunteers and be forever present at the Vietnam Veterans Memorial. The recipient of The Libby Hatch Special Recognition Award is selected by members of the Hatch family based on written and oral recommendations made by past and present volunteers, National Park Service Rangers, Vietnam veterans, visitors to The Wall and any other interested parties. The award is presented each year during the annual Libby Hatch Volunteer Appreciation Luncheon. Past recipients include: Lee Adriani, Frank Bosch, Red Flegal, Charlie Harootunian and Sid George.

Memorial Fund staffers Libby Hatch and Holly Rotondi take a break after the Veterans Day 1997 ceremony.

Courtesy of William Lecky

VVMF © Frederick E. Hart/VVMF 1984

The Three Servicemen statue was added to the Vietnam Veterans Memorial in 1984.

HOW TO BECOME A VOLUNTEER

While there are a host of volunteers, there is always a need for more dedicated hands and hearts. "Living in a world of decreased government resources, these public-private partnerships are important, especially as they affect parks, both our national and local parks," explained Scruggs. "Citizens have to grab the bull by the horns, and that's what the volunteers do at the Memorial."

"Being a volunteer is important to me. You might as well just cut my heart out if I couldn't volunteer," said Harootunian. "And there's so much that needs to be done there. Many times, people go down and there isn't enough help. That used to bother me a lot. It used to be hard for me to leave, but I had to realize there was only so much that I could do."

"A lot of new volunteers are recruited by current volunteers," said Rotondi. But, anyone who is interested can give their time. (*For more information on how to become a volunteer, see Appendix 4.*)

Sadly, a few weeks after being interviewed for this book, Vietnam Veterans Memorial volunteer Lee Adriani died suddenly. She will be missed by her friends at the Memorial Fund and the National Park Service and her fellow volunteers at the Memorial, as well as all of the visitors who benefited from her warmth and compassion.

Daniel Arant

A military unit out for a run slows when they walk past The Wall.

After the dedication ceremony on November 13, 1982, visitors crowd against The Wall to get a closer look.

Daniel Arant

Donna Prince

Daniel Arant

WILLIAM L LOGAN · DUANE CRUM · GARY L HOLIAN · ERIC S KEE
JOHN M RYDLEWICZ · GAIL L STRICKLAND · JOHN C THOMPSON
AN Jr · MARK H EATON · JOHN F PEPIN · FLOYD W KOTEWA Jr · HAYWOOD RODG
B CHASTAIN · SCOTT T GRABER · VERNON HART · LEROY REID Jr · JOHN W KENNE
ANTONIO T TOSA · ARTHUR G DENTN · WILLIE C KUYKENDALL · JOHN L BRAN
A BROWDER Jr · DANIEL E GOODIN · CHRISTOPHER G MORBITZER · BRUCE MOR
MAN · JOHNNY E JONES · MICHAEL · DRY · JAMES J WINSON · TROY E BRANTL
EROON · DAVID W FRADY · DWIGH · OWELL · VIRGIL J BATES Jr · WILLIAM E LAM

(This page and opposite page) Among the more than 100,000 items left at The Wall are boots, hats, medals and photographs.

CHARLES E HODGE · JOHN W HOGAN · SAMUEL B
DONALD E JONES · GUY T JONES · STEPHEN C JON
RICHARD A KOSKI · JIMMY M LOGAN · WILLIAM T M
KENNETH C MOORE · DOUGLAS N McKENZIE II · FR
WILLIAM T PUFFENBARGER · MELVIN R RANSON · GA
LS P ROGAN · MICHAEL D ROLFE · SAMUEL J RUM
LIP E SEXTON · MICHAEL A SHRAMKO · LARRY R
NIE STEPHENS · GEORGE W STORZ · JOHN J SULI
E K WILSON · DONALD W VAN FLEET · RODOLFO
H WILLIAMS · TERRY A WILLIAMS · JOHN M TOMM
RY S BAKER · JAMES R BATEMAN · WILLIAM H BECK
BERT L CLEWLOW · ROBERT J COMSTOCK · MAURIC
ANCIS R HITTINGER Jr · JOHN E HOOD · DONALD R
LVIN R LEAVELL · PATRICK D MORIARTY · JOSEPH ES
CHARD N PROCIDA · STEPHEN J RAGO · JAMES RIVER

VVMF

THE VIETNAM VETERANS MEMORIAL COLLECTION

On any given day, in any type of weather, a visitor to the Memorial will notice that along the base of the black granite walls lay items left by other visitors. Much like the names on The Wall, these offerings have become a phenomenon of the Vietnam Veterans Memorial. "People were leaving items before the dedication of The Wall," explained Duery Felton, a Vietnam veteran and curator of the Vietnam Veterans Memorial Collection at the National Park Service's Museum Resource Center (MRCE) in Landover, Md.

The practice of leaving items at The Wall began in 1982, when someone placed a Purple Heart in the concrete being poured during the Memorial's construction. According to legend, the surviving brother of a U.S. Navy pilot who was killed in Vietnam approached the construction crew as they were pouring cement for the foundation. He asked the crew's permission to place the Purple Heart in the freshly poured cement. After he dropped it in, he saluted, did an "about face" and walked away. For many, this story exemplifies the reasons why people proclaim that "the Memorial has a heart."

But, the Purple Heart was only the beginning. Visitors who tried to glimpse the Memorial often left items at the site near the construction fences. One of the National Park Service (NPS) maintenance workers noticed the items and began collecting them and placing them in a nearby storage facility. As more items were left, NPS staff joined in collecting them. Initially, Felton said, there was a belief that people might return to reclaim the items.

"It was unheard of, people leaving unsolicited items at a national memorial site for any length of time," he recalled. The items were not simply the traditional wreath or bouquet of flowers left at gravesites or memorials. Instead, they included notes, photographs, military medals, dog tags and patches.

"Early on, there was a large preponderance of military objects," Felton explained. The items were usually small and could easily fit in a person's pocket, making them easy to transport.

Even as NPS gathered and stored the items, it wasn't clear what should be done with them. No one had a sense as to how long people might continue to leave things at The Wall. And there was a growing list of questions: Why are so many people leaving things? What do these offerings mean? And who are the offerings for, those on The Wall or those still living?

Many have tried to answer these questions. Kristin Hass, an instructor at the University of Michigan, wrote this explanation in her 1998 book, *Carried to The Wall*:

"People carrying their things to the Wall are answering, and asking, questions about society's obligations to its soldiers. After other recent wars, bringing flags to the grave sites of soldiers on official memorial holidays was an important part of paying homage to fallen soldiers for their sacrifice; the flags marked an honored memory of the dead and were a reminder of the debt that nation owed to its soldiers. This debt was not paid after Vietnam, and bringing a medal or a lock of hair or 59 cents or a political sticker to the Vietnam Veterans Memorial is an intervention in the public crisis of memory spurred by the nation's failure to pay it. The giving of these gifts is a powerful symbolic response to this betrayal; all of the medals and money and fetishized pieces of bodies and political iconography, taken together, are a…collective negotiation about the problem of the memory of the deaths and the war."

"When we built the Memorial, no one foresaw this happening," said Jan Scruggs, founder and president of the Memorial Fund. "Our goal was to help the nation remember and pay tribute to all who served and sacrificed in Vietnam. No one anticipated that The Wall would become a place where visitors would leave tokens of their love, esteem and remembrance."

THE MUSEUM RESOURCE CENTER

Pam West, director of the Museum Resource Center in Landover, Md., watched with interest as the assortment of memorabilia grew. MRCE, a facility of the National Park Service, is home to 44 collections related to NPS sites in the National Capital Region and over 1 million archeological artifacts.

Yet this grouping of items was unlike any other because the objects were not being selected by a curator to represent an important moment or event in time. Instead, it was the individual visitors to The Wall who laid objects at its base who were deciding what held significance.

As time passed, West and others recognized that they were witnessing an important phenomenon. She proposed that the objects be considered a formal collection and be accorded the same deference as those from any other historical site. In 1986, permission was granted for the creation of the Vietnam Veterans Memorial Collection, which includes any nonperishable items left at The Wall and the other elements of the Vietnam Veterans Memorial, which include the Three Servicemen statue, the flagpole, the Vietnam Women's Memorial and the In Memory plaque.

With the collection acknowledged in a more formal way and after several years of studying different ways to handle it, MRCE implemented processes for collecting and cataloguing items. Each night, NPS rangers gather and inventory the items. In bad weather, NPS volunteers may also collect objects in order to protect them. There is a temporary holding facility at the ranger kiosk near The Wall where items can be held before being transferred to MRCE.

The Museum Resource Center is a state-of-the-art, climate-controlled museum facility that is not open to the public, although MRCE staff create exhibits for display at other museums.

Once at MRCE, items are treated as part of a historical collection. They are dated, numbered, catalogued and placed in storage as if they were extremely old and valuable. What makes the collection so unique is that it is uncensored. Nonperishable items are archived without judgment regarding their value or contribution to the greater collection. The mere appearance of an item at The Wall affords it meaning.

"This collection is different, especially when you understand the significance of this object to this person," said Felton. One example is the collection's 3rd place karate competition medal. Traditionally, a medal might only be included in a collection if it were rare or made from a valuable material such as gold. The 3rd place medal left at the Memorial has meaning because of all that it might represent.

"The person [who won this medal] had to give up TV or recreation activities to practice karate and to come in 3rd place. By leaving their karate medal here, it's not that it was made of a noble material, but it is noble when you understand what it meant to the person that left it behind after making personal sacrifices," said Felton.

In the instance of medals, the stories of sacrifice and commitment are just as poignant. Numerous Purple Hearts have been added to the collection, since that first one was dropped into the concrete. "All Purple Hearts share the same configuration," explained Felton. "But to place 100 on a table [is to] realize that I'm looking at a minimum of 100 individual stories."

(Previous page) Many remembrances are left at The Wall at Christmas time.

(Right) Visitors often touch the names they are seeking.

LEROY LAWSON

All photos this page by Daniel Arant

(Previous page and above) Many of the items in the Vietnam Veterans Memorial Collection have meanings known only to whose who left them.

ALL THINGS BIG AND SMALL

Over the years, the nature of the items left at The Wall has evolved and changed. "We think word was getting out that we were collecting and preserving these items for perpetuity," Felton explained. "People started to leave items [sealed] in plastic bags or laminated. Items were getting larger and more sophisticated."

One of the more unique items was a Harley-Davidson motorcycle. "A volunteer called and said 'There's a motorcycle down here,'" recalled Felton. "The rangers allowed a photograph to be taken of the bike by The Wall, but then they wanted it moved an appropriate distance so as not to obstruct flow of traffic or risk the motorcycle damaging The Wall."

Certain items, like the motorcycle, are removed before day's end to guard against theft, to protect The Wall and even to protect visitors. "If the rangers or volunteers feel uncomfortable seeing something lying there, they know they can pick it up to care for it," added Felton.

One veteran called Felton to let him know that he was going to leave a rifle at the Memorial. "He wanted people to get an idea of the type of armaments used by the Viet Cong," explained Felton. "I told him, 'I'm going to give you the phone number to the kiosk because I don't want you to leave it at The Wall.'" Felton then called the kiosk to let the rangers know to expect the item.

Another unusual object was a large storm door made to fit a commercial building that had been painted on both sides. One side was a landscaped war scene; the other was an homage to POWs and MIAs. "But the door wasn't manufactured to be a canvas," explained Felton. So the MRCE staff took special steps to preserve and protect it.

Many items left at The Wall have the power to make political or social commentary. "This is a public soapbox," said Felton. With the Memorial's location in Washington, D.C. and the city's power as a visitor's center, any time there are concerts, parades, marches or protests, items related to that event will be carried to The Wall.

The most common items left at The Wall are notes and letters. In the beginning, notes seemed to be spontaneous. "A note would be written on a paper bag from one of the museum bookstores," recalled Felton. Visitors overcome with emotion felt compelled to leave their thoughts behind. Then, as personal computers became popular, letters were typed and printed beforehand, then placed at The Wall.

"Early on, we knew the military holidays would be active," explained Felton. The staff learned to expect a surge in the collection at Memorial Day and Veterans Day. Then, they discovered that items were also appearing on family holidays, such as Thanksgiving.

"We started to notice that there were occasion cards being left on holidays, personal days, birthdays and anniversaries," Felton noted. In many instances, people return year after year on the same date to leave cards marking special remembrances.

One of the most memorable items in the Collection is a Harley-Davidson motorcycle made specifically to be brought to The Wall.

On Father's Day, yellow roses represent those service members who are missing in action.

Daniel Arant

Leroy Lawson

A little boy examines The Wall.

THE THOUGHT BEHIND EACH ITEM

The sentiments and mystery behind each item make the collection especially intriguing. Hours could be spent contemplating the intention behind each offering. Jack Wheeler, a veteran and the former chairman of the Memorial Fund, recalled visiting The Wall shortly after a snowstorm. "Everything was white, except for this small streak of color sticking out of the snow. It was a bridal bouquet," he recalled. "That's all there was. Why a bridal bouquet? I thought maybe it was the daughter saying, 'Dad, I got married; here's my bouquet.'"

Occasionally, the meaning behind an item is discovered. One man always leaves baseball souvenirs accompanied by his unit's insignia. The veteran explained to Felton that the baseballs are for all who have missed seeing the greats of today play the game. "When I see his unit's insignia along with a baseball, I know it's from him," said Felton. The collection contains numerous baseball cards, gloves, bats and balls. Who knows what each of them might represent?

When there is no explanation to accompany an item, the MRCE staff attempts to archive objects with any known facts in order to provide context. This is particularly useful when the collection is on display for the public. "Some of it is conjecture," Felton said. "For example, we have M&Ms in this collection. The history of M&Ms goes back to WWII. It was used for field energy because they wouldn't melt on a soldier's trigger finger." M&Ms were also included in care packages sent to service members. This type of anecdotal information might accompany a displayed bag of M&Ms if no information was supplied by the donor.

THE COLLECTION ON DISPLAY

In October 1992, the Smithsonian Institution in Washington, D.C. opened an exhibit at the Museum of American History that contained items from the Vietnam Veterans Memorial Collection. Titled "Personal Legacy: The Healing of a Nation," it contained more than 1,500 objects. It was the first time that the National Park Service and the Smithsonian Institution worked together to develop a major exhibition.

They selected objects that were representative of items left at The Wall, hoping to share the depth of the collection. They included many military-related items, including combat boots, medals and dog tags, as well as more personal items like teddy bears.

Between 75,000 to 100,000 people visited the exhibit in its first six months. According to Felton, the lines to get in to see the collection were so long that the Smithsonian had to place guards at the end to shut them down well in advance of the museum's closing time.

In the early days of the exhibit's opening, many of the cards and letters were tucked inside special protective sleeves and put on display in glass cases. Visitors to the exhibit would take their time reading the heartfelt messages of love and loss. Unfortunately, that caused the lines to move exceedingly slow and to grow painfully long.

At one point, Felton was called to the museum to clean the display cases. The visitors who strained to read the notes behind the glass, many of whom were crying, left it streaked, smudged and smeared. To correct both issues, the notes and letters were copied and placed in three-ring binders for easier access in an area that did not interrupt museum traffic flow.

Originally, the exhibit was slated to be open for six months. Due to its overwhelming popularity, it remained open for 11 years.

Daniel Arant

In addition to the display at the Smithsonian Institution, exhibits have also been displayed at the Imperial War Museum in London, England; the Museum of Our National Heritage in Lexington, Mass.; The Gerald R. Ford Presidential Library in Grand Rapids, Mich.; and the Department of Veterans Affairs in Washington, D.C., New York, Los Angeles and Houston, Texas. An exhibit at the Jersey Explorers Children Museum, "Vietnam Memories: Stories Left at The Wall," was produced in conjunction with the New Jersey Youth Corps and Ameri-Corps at Jersey City State College.

"This collection receives more access requests than all the other collections combined," Felton explained. When he works with organizations that request an exhibit, he takes into account the group's unique focus and interests when culling objects for display.

"For the Department of Veterans Affairs [VA], the things I would lend them aren't the same as I would lend a children's museum. For the VA, we had a Tupperware container with upper and lower dentures [in it] with a note attached," Felton recalled. In essence, the note read that since the Department of Veterans Affairs had provided the veteran with his final, permanent implant, then he would no longer need the dentures. To Felton, they seemed a particularly fitting item to include in an exhibit for the VA.

But few organizations have the ability to sponsor an exhibit. "One of the things we want to do when we get time is to do a traveling photo exhibition," said Felton. This approach would satisfy the need in areas that don't have museum venue space and enable more people to experience the collection.

100,000 ITEMS AND GROWING

In December 2006, the Vietnam Veterans Memorial Collection reached the 100,000 mark, although it is impossible to determine which particular item might have qualified as the milestone.

"Imagine a leather jacket that someone has left," explained Felton. "It has buttons, pins, decorations, and in the pockets are receipts from the hotels and restaurants they went to during their trip. So, is the jacket counted as one item or 40?" For these reasons, the Museum Resource Center uses the term "assemblage" to address a group of items left at The Wall together—for example, a pair of boots with a letter and dog tag.

Sometimes, the process of cataloguing assemblage items is daunting. "I have a Marine assemblage that will take two months to catalogue," Felton said. "It's a helmet mounted on top of a 4-foot-by-4-foot piece of wood with a reproduction of a service ribbon, a letter on the bottom [and] an estimated 200 to 300 dog tags." Each item must be tagged with a unique number, documented with the name of the person cataloguing the item and noted with any special markings and descriptions.

"This collection is challenging because it's so dynamic that it's difficult to keep up," he added.

Objects from the first 100,000 items collected at The Wall will be featured in rotating exhibits at the Vietnam Veterans Memorial Center, a facility that will be built underground on the National Mall near the Vietnam Veterans Memorial. *(For more information about the Memorial Center, see Chapter 4.)*

LIGHTING THE WAY

By developing this collection, the National Park Service has set the standard for modern documentary collections. "We're the flagship guiding the efforts for other memorials," said Felton.

NPS has provided technical guidance to the curatorial staff for Oklahoma City, Columbine, Flight 93, "9-11" and other similar memorials. In fact, West and Felton have been consulted on international memorial collections as well, including one for the Madrid train bombing. That involves helping them contemplate important issues, such as what should be collected and for how long.

Felton admits that financial concerns may limit how long some memorials can collect items left there. "For us," he added, "there's no 'sunset clause.'"

(Previous page) A tribute is left for POW Roque Versace, who was killed in captivity.

(Right) A mother holds her son's photograph next to his name, November 1982.

Two girls make name rubbings at the apex of The Wall.

A veteran touches a name.

THE PEOPLE'S COLLECTION
BY PAMELA WEST

Who would have thought of the general public as curators of a major museum collection — curators whose job is to choose objects which will be placed in a collection that will be preserved and interpreted for perpetuity. This is exactly what has happened at the Vietnam Veterans Memorial.

Most museum objects are collected because they relate to a special event, person or natural wonder. The museum curator selects these specific objects to tell a story. However, in this case, it is the public who collects and leaves the objects at The Wall. While these objects may have a central theme of the Vietnam War or generation, the power of the Memorial and the individual stories behind these objects is really the focus of this collection.

The National Park Service certainly never thought of starting a collection when it entered into an agreement with the Vietnam Veterans Memorial Fund, who were going to build a memorial to those who had served in Vietnam and those who made the ultimate sacrifice. At that time, we were concerned only with receiving a memorial that was to heal the wounds suffered during the Vietnam era, of the nation and its individuals, whether they were pro-war or anti-war.

The public began leaving "things" at the Memorial which later became known as memorabilia. These "things" do not fit the standard definition of artifacts or historical objects, terms used to describe something over 50 years old. But whether they fit the definition or not, this was the start of one of the most unique and interesting museum collections that the National Park Service would deal with in the 1980s and 1990s.

In order to better understand this collection, we ask ourselves many questions, such as: why is The Wall so powerful and what makes people bring things and leave them?

The Wall has a power that is felt differently by each visitor who comes to the Memorial. The same questions continue to be asked. Why does it compel people to come and leave things? Why are some left spontaneously and others prepared at home, brought to Washington, or in many cases sent to Washington with someone who happens to be going to the Memorial? Why do some people bring things to leave and then find themselves unable to do so?

The answers to all the questions that we and others ask can only be speculated, and they might never be known. But as long as people still come to The Wall, whether they leave "things" or not, it fulfills the purpose for which this Memorial was originally intended: to heal a nation. This memorial works for it was created by the people, paid for by the people, the collection was made by the people, and the Smithsonian exhibit was funded by the people. This is truly the people's collection.

Pamela West is the director of the Museum Resource Center, which houses and cares for the Vietnam Veterans Memorial Collection.

Members of the U.S. Marine Corps pay their respects at The Wall.

Tom Esprin

JOHN L GEOGHEGAN · WILLIE F GODBOLDT · ROBER
AMES · CARL E HARRIS
RRINGTON · JO
DOUGLAS H
RE · SAMUEL L McD
· EDDIE LEE POUGH
NNIER · LEONARD W S
CKER · WILLIAM T VI
ER · JOHN R ACKE
N · EDDIE BRO
REEN · RO
RICH
KENNETH C BOLI
ENNETH E R BURCH
· DANNY E CARLTON
LLINS · RONALD C C
EED ·
OTI

Naval Academy midshipmen pause to look at things left at The Wall.

Daniel Arant

Gen. Peter Pace, a Vietnam veteran, was the first Marine to be appointed chairman of the Joint Chiefs of Staff. He spoke at The Wall on Veterans Day 2005.

141

Mark Segal © 1984

A Special Visitor:
The Commander in Chief Pays Tribute

During the nearly week-long series of activities that led up to the 10th anniversary of the Memorial in November 1992, one of the most important events was the reading of the names. This had never before been done at The Wall.

After a few dignitaries and VIPs started off the reading to the waiting press, the cameras were turned off and the really important people began the nearly 72-hour process. These were the people with strong, personal connections to The Wall. The audience for this emotional event varied by the time of day, from several hundred in the pleasant daylight hours to several dozen in the cold, damp, early November pre-dawn hours.

It was after 11 p.m. one evening. The crowds were small, and the scene was peaceful, until a group of well-dressed individuals caused a disruption. A young lady who had signed up to read some names was being asked by these strangers if she would share her names with "the president." This lady was not from the Washington, D.C. area and responded by asking what he was the president of. The presidential handler made it clear that he was referring to the 41st president of the United States, George H.W. Bush. Still, she resisted, because the names she was reading were special to her.

Hearing her response, the president edged past his assistant and commented to her directly. Basically, he said: "I don't want to read your special names, but are there any on your list who you don't know personally that you might share with me?"

The answer was yes. So, when the time came, this volunteer, along with President George H.W. Bush and First Lady Barbara Bush, proceeded onto the stage to read the list of names together. At this time of night, the seats were normally fairly empty, but when the president stepped up to read, every seat seemed to be magically filled. The darkness was suddenly bright with camera flashes and television lighting.

But the president was not there for publicity. He raised his hand in a halting motion and asked the assembled press to turn off their lights and cameras. "I'm not here to read for the press," he said. "I'm here to read for these heroes on The Wall." They complied, and he read the brief list of names. Then he thanked the volunteer who shared her names with him and left the stage, staying nearby for a little while afterward to talk with the volunteers and veterans who, like him, had braved the elements to pay tribute to fallen heroes.

Ten years later, another VIP guest visited The Wall during the quiet hours. It was the morning of Veterans Day 2002, the 20th anniversary of The Wall.

Preparations start early for these ceremonies. At 6:30 a.m., Memorial Fund Vice President of Programs Holly Rotondi was dismayed to find that the crews setting up the chairs and sound system for the afternoon ceremony were being denied access to the area in front of The Wall. And then she saw why.

"Around 7:30 on a cold, rainy morning, when no one was there to see him, President George W. Bush came to The Wall to pay his respects," she remembered. He lingered for a few moments, left his presidential coin, then talked with some volunteers before going on his way. No members of the press were present.

In the case of the father and the son, both presidents, those who witnessed these private visits were left with a warm feeling. What a great country this is where the highest leader in the land can occasionally join with everyday citizens for a common purpose: to remember those who gave their lives in the service of this country.

CHAPTER 7
THE IMPACT OF THE
VIETNAM VETERANS MEMORIAL

On the days when ceremonies are held, many more visitors than normal come to The Wall.

Daniel Arant

THE IMPACT OF THE VIETNAM VETERANS MEMORIAL

Over the past 25 years, the Vietnam Veterans Memorial has had a wide-ranging impact on our nation. It has the power to reflect and to urge reflection. It can prompt uniquely personal experiences, yet move masses to tears. It has altered our perception of historical events as strongly as it has influenced how we view events of today. It is a hard, impenetrable acknowledgement of loss that beckons the tender touch of a name. Ultimately, it has become an undeniable symbol of American sacrifice, honor and healing.

THE HISTORY OF MEMORIALS

American memorialization has evolved over time. As our culture shifts, so too does our idea of what to commemorate. Historians point to specific events and trends that have changed how and what we memorialize. The Vietnam Veterans Memorial is one of the influential markers on their timeline.

American memorialization practices began to change during the Civil War. Before that, war memorials paid tribute to triumphs or to powerful leaders, with little attention paid to the soldier who fought the battle. But, according to Kristin Ann Hass, author of *Carried to The Wall,* memorialization efforts after the 1860s began to articulate the connection between the individual soldier and the nation.

She cited what happened at Gettysburg in 1863 as a cause for this. During the battle, the bodies of the dead were hastily buried. But afterward, local citizens dug up the bodies and searched for clues to their identities. The dead were then reburied with grave markers in what would become Soldiers' National Cemetery.

Gettysburg was the first time in our country's history that the individual soldier's sacrifice was acknowledged and honored. "New traditions created at Gettysburg radically transformed ideas about what to do with the bodies and the memory of the war dead and, in turn, transformed the making of national memory in the United States and Europe," Hass explained.

One of the greatest impacts resulting from this shift was the change in viewing soldiers as citizens rather than merely as mercenaries. Citizen soldiers had families who loved and missed them, and the nation began to grieve their loss.

After World War I, memorials focused more on the issue of civic beautification. No longer was a stone memorial or marker sufficient. Citizens wanted to honor those who died by bettering the very communities for which they served.

After World War II and the Korean War, this concept expanded. "This practical turn in the work of memorializing was an expression of a genuine commitment to the material expectations of postwar nationalism in the United States," Hass explained. "The people who wanted memorials did not want to waste time and money on symbolic stone that did not advance the prosperity of a victorious nation. Americans seemed to want to reap the benefits of the free world for which they had sacrificed so much. So they built football fields, playgrounds and highways and called them war memorials."

With the proliferation of these "living memorials," there remained the desire to remember the individual fallen soldier. In many towns across the country, names of those who died in World War II were added to plaques at local World War I memorials.

When the time came to remember the Vietnam War and those who served, memorialization was further clouded by the country's confusion over the war. There was no clear consensus regarding the war's purpose or meaning. The country was struggling with how to grieve as a community.

"Commemorating the war and the deaths required giving new shape to the broken meanings of the war. It required a reimagination of the nation," Hass wrote.

That reimagination was made possible by Lin's design. As she described in her winning design proposal: "It is up to each

The presentation of names honors individual sacrifice in a stunning and powerful way.

VVMF

VVMF

Sara McVicker

People come to The Wall alone and in groups.

(Bottom left) Four nurses who served together in Vietnam meet at The Wall.

individual to resolve or to come to terms with this loss. For death is in the end a personal and private matter and the area containing this within the memorial is a quiet place, meant for personal reflection and private reckoning."

This approach was a vast departure from the memorials on the National Mall, which were white, symbolic and triumphant in nature. In a May 21, 2000 article in *TIME* magazine, Roger Rosenblatt wrote: "Statues, tombs, arches, pyramids, obelisks: all have stood for abstractions such as heroism, sacrifice and valor." All of the monuments and memorials on the National Mall prior to The Wall featured this type of classical architectural design. They were also massively vertical, rising up in grandeur.

"[The Vietnam Veterans Memorial] created a new paradigm for memorials in Washington, possibly nationally and internationally, because of the fact that it was so different," said Thomas Luebke, secretary of the Commission of Fine Arts, speaking at a March 26, 2007 panel discussion on "The Vietnam Veterans Memorial: The Changing Face of Memorials and the National Mall."

According to Luebke, the Memorial was distinct in three critical ways. It was located on the National Mall, whereas the majority of previous war memorials were local in nature. It was horizontal rather than vertical. And, its departure from traditional memorial design approaches — its use of high-polished black granite in a landscaped solution void of obelisks and columns — altered the architectural language.

Lin's simple, horizontal, black chevron shape cut deep into the earth made a dramatically different statement, yet it also incorporated many of the major trends in memorialization. Its presentation of names honors individual sacrifice in a stunning and powerful way. The Memorial epitomizes the notion behind the citizen soldier.

Its location on the National Mall, on such hallowed ground between the Washington Monument and the Lincoln Memorial, speaks to its sacred and important purpose. "Putting the Vietnam Veterans Memorial alongside long-revered national symbols...gives the VVM a prominent context, psychological, physical and symbolic," wrote Ken Petress and Andrew King in their paper, *Speaking in Many Voices: The Vietnam Veterans Memorial*. Its design and tranquil, park-like setting serve as symbols of civic beautification and living memorial efforts.

So, the Vietnam Veterans Memorial advanced major trends in memorialization, while it also forged important new concepts involving contemplation, reflection and reconciliation that further shaped our ideas of how, what and why we commemorate. And it accomplished all of those aspects without commenting politically on the war itself.

The interpretive aspect of its design influenced a great number of other memorials. "Today, design puts the responsibility to make meaning on the part of the people who are visiting the memorial," said Hass.

This can be seen in the Oklahoma City National Memorial, where 168 bronze-and-glass chairs honor the 168 people killed in the bombing of the Alfred P. Murrah Building. Who are the chairs for? Do they represent the people who died as they sat at their desks that awful morning of April 19, 1995? Does a visitor sit in a chair to peer into the reflective pool and remember? Or to be closer to the dead?

There are no definitive answers, which has been the point of modern memorial design since The Wall. "Older memorials used to honor permanence. Newer ones treat permanence as an illusion," Rosenblatt wrote in his *TIME* article.

The Korean War Veterans and the World War II Memorials, both built afterward, are explicit responses to the Vietnam Veterans Memorial. "The Wall made memorials matter again," said Hass. "The ones built since have been about rewriting what it means to be a soldier on the National Mall. The Mall is sacred ground. Who gets ground means who gets to forge the history and what will be said."

Additionally, there was great significance in the incorporation of the Three Servicemen statue with The Wall. As Edward Smith, director of American Studies at American University, pointed out during the panel discussion on "The Vietnam Veterans Memorial: The Changing Face of Memorials and the National Mall" on March 26, 2007: "You have this representational form [the statue] married with this abstraction [The Wall] and of course with the names. It's such a wonderful blend. It sets the tone for so many other memorials."

Some experts say that, following the Vietnam Veterans Memorial, there was a swell in "statue and wall" designs, as seen in both the Korean War Veterans and the Franklin Delano Roosevelt Memorials. (Technically, the FDR Memorial design was selected in 1974, although according to an April 27, 1997 article by Doug Struck in *The Washington Post*, the design was revised considerably over the next 20 years until the 1994 groundbreaking.)

The Korean War Veterans Memorial features statues of fighting men on patrol, coupled with a granite mural of over 2,000 sandblasted photographs honoring those who provided supply, medical, spiritual and fire support to the frontline units. All of these elements point toward the Pool of Remembrance, where the sacrifices of those who died can be contemplated.

The recently dedicated Air Force Memorial also combines modern elements — three soaring 270-foot-high spires — with a traditional bronze statue. According to Ross Perot Jr., a key

Terry Adams, National Park Service

The Vietnam Veterans Memorial has an important place on the National Mall.

The Korean War Veterans Memorial and the FDR Memorial use the "statue and wall" design popularized by the Vietnam Veterans Memorial.

participant in the effort to build the Air Force Memorial, the statue plays a significant role in the visitor's experience. "The Air Force Memorial is so tall it would be difficult for people to have their photo taken at it," he explained. "But they can at the Honor Guard statue, and that's where everybody gets their photo taken."

The design of the World War II Memorial is a bit more like its older predecessors, with a few modern elements. It is much grander in size and scale than other recent memorials, but manages to balance both classical and modernist styles of architecture while incorporating the contemplative element of large water fountains and pools.

Similar to The Wall, many modern memorials also invite the visitor to interact. "It's intimate abstraction," explained John Baky, Connelly Library director at La Salle University in Philadelphia, Pa. "At the Korean War Memorial, you can walk in between the soldiers and see fear on their faces; it has a kinetic quality."

"These monuments are known as destination monuments," explained Jim Percoco, author and history educator. "In order to understand the experience, you have to enter into the memorial space. For the Vietnam Veterans Memorial, you go down, off the street level, where it is quiet and sobering; whereas if you go to the Lincoln Memorial on any weekday, you'll hear a lot more noise. It's a different experience because of the design."

Those qualities have endured. And, in February 2007, the American Institute of Architects awarded its 25 Year Award to the Vietnam Veterans Memorial for architectural design that has stood the test of time. Harry Robinson, a Vietnam veteran, long-time Memorial Fund board member and a dean emeritus at Howard University, noted that the award is generally selected during the second day of jury deliberations. In this particular instance, the jury unanimously awarded the 25 Year Award to the Vietnam Veterans Memorial on its first vote.

Many feel its power is in its design. "It creates a magical moment of the living and the dead touching that's still as potent as the first time you saw it," said Luebke. "That's the challenge you have [for memorials], for it to really be meaningful: it's part location, part design, then hopefully you get a magical combination somewhere in between."

The World War II Memorial (above) and the Air Force Memorial (right) are both grander in size and scale than other recent memorials.

Terry Adams, National Park Service

Vietnam Veterans of America Color Guards stand at attention during the 20th anniversary ceremonies, Veterans Day 2002.

Both photos by VVMF

A veteran remembers his fallen comrade.

Sara McVicker

A former Navy corpsman stands with his wife in front of the panel containing the names of the Marines who died in the firefight in which he was badly injured.

Tom Estrin

The Gold Star Wives of America lay a wreath at the Memorial, Veterans Day 2003.

A Variety of Audiences

As individual as our memories and emotions are, so too are our interactions with The Wall. Part of its tremendous power is in how it can be many things to many people.

"Memorials don't necessarily remember anything; they invent something. They produce from the chaotic, multiple events of the past. They exist to produce digestible meaning," Hass said.

However, "The Wall doesn't quite go that far," she added. "It's left open, which might be one reason people are so engaged with it. Its reflective quality means people can go back. You use what the Memorial gives you to make meaning."

According to Henry Hattemer in an article posted on Editio, an online academic publisher, four distinct groups come to The Wall: the typical tourist or "casual" visitor with no personal connection to the war; the visitor who may have known someone who fought or died in the war; the soldier from any era or branch of the military; and the Vietnam veteran. The Vietnam Veterans Memorial manages to speak to each of these groups in different ways.

To the tourist, says Hattemer, The Wall is either an educator or a reminder of the great cost of war. The soldier who visits The Wall "is there to remember respectfully his colleagues who perished working the same job that he wakes up to every morning," Hattemer wrote. "He shares a certain brotherhood with every single name on The Wall."

The Vietnam veteran who visits recalls far more direct and personal experiences related to the war. Of course, the veteran is also prompted to remember fallen friends and comrades.

"While the Vietnam Veterans Memorial most obviously pays tribute to the memory of those who died during the war, it is a central icon for the veterans," Marita Sturken wrote in her article, "The Wall, the Screen, and the Image: The Vietnam Veterans Memorial," which appeared in the 1991 publication *Representations*. "It has been noted that the Memorial has given them a place: one that recognizes their identities, a place at which to congregate and from which to speak. Hence, the Memorial is as much about survival as it is about mourning the dead."

In their paper, Petress and King offered a similar conclusion, in that The Wall "offered all parties most of what they wanted and even more of what they needed. A greater sense of peace over the Vietnam War and its participants now pervades the land."

A veteran of the 1st Marine Division mourns by The Wall.

"Dust Off" was the radio call sign used by the helicopter medical evacuation units.

Sara McVicker

Tom Estrin

Tom Estrin

(Background) Veterans carry a wreath to The Wall on Veterans Day 2003.

(Top inset) A woman veteran attends the 10th anniversary of the dedication of the Vietnam Women's Memorial, November 2003.

(Bottom inset) American Gold Star Mothers Ann Herd and Emogene Cupp attend a ceremony.

HOW WE REMEMBER

History is not merely the dates, names and chronology of facts surrounding an event or person. It is a tapestry of facts woven together with the threads of memory, imagination and interpretation.

"If we think about history as a way of shaping how people understand themselves and the society in which they live, its importance becomes more obvious. Why we dress the way we do, why we speak in a certain way and why we celebrate particular holidays all are influenced by events that took place in the past," wrote historian Spencer R. Crew, National Museum of American History Smithsonian Institution, in an essay for the American Historical Association (AHA) Web site.

Consequently, historians are tasked with creating meaningful narratives around significant events and people, narratives that evolve over time as our culture, understanding and perceptions change.

For those focused on developing a narrative about the Vietnam War, the Memorial has served as a conduit to conversations, recollections and interpretations about the war experience and its aftermath.

"The construction of an identity for the veterans since their return from the war has become the most present and continuing narrative of the memorial," Sturken wrote. "The central theme of this narrative is the way the veterans had been invisible and without voice before the memorial's construction and the subsequent interest in discussing the war." Those discussions not only help to shape the historical narrative, but also help society to grasp and synthesize particularly painful events.

Connelly Library Director John Baky explained the powerful role that The Wall is playing in this process. "With a lot of traumatic historical events, people have a great need to 're-remember' in ways that allow them to be comfortable," he said. "If they have to live with the reality of certain events, it becomes almost too much, and they reject it outright. [Instead] we try to remember in a way that we can digest it all.

"The Wall reinvents itself, and it also reinvents what people are trying to remember," Baky added. "The intensity of the desire to remember or re-remember the Vietnam War is almost without end."

A mother finds her son's name.

Edward A. Leskin

Memorial Fund Founder and President Jan Scruggs reads a letter left at The Wall.

Daniel Arant

MANY FORMS OF HEALING

When Jan Scruggs first conceived of building a memorial to honor those who had served and sacrificed in the Vietnam War, he knew there was a great need for healing. The veterans, so long ignored, needed to be recognized. The families, so long in pain, needed to grieve. The country, so long divided, needed to be reunited.

Some kind of national recognition was necessary.

"Without memorialization, there's a very dangerous effect, the notion that if you don't grieve properly, you're putting yourself in great jeopardy for all sorts of things," explained Baky. "You can have a culture or a nation which can enter into a depression just like a person can. That happens when the grief process is short-circuited. That's what accounted for the tears, for the masses crying at The Wall."

"When I first heard of the plans to build the Vietnam Veterans Memorial, I thought, 'It's about time that those who served in Vietnam are being recognized,'" former President George H. W. Bush said. "As you know, many veterans of that war returned home to abuse and outrageous disrespect. I was very happy when The Wall was proposed and that wrong was going to be righted."

"It boils down to the notion of honoring what's represented by the individual names," said Baky. With so many names, there is a real sense of grief and sadness.

"The first time I visited, like everyone else I believe, I was struck by the power of the names on The Wall," said former Senator Bob Dole. "I believe the Memorial overwhelms anyone who visits because of its design, but in addition to the overwhelming nature of the names, it is also a very beautiful tribute to their sacrifice."

The Wall granted us, as a nation and as individuals, permission to talk openly about the war, about our lost loved ones, about our emotions in all their visceral incarnations. In the article "Pilgrimage to the Wall," featured in *Christian Century* magazine, Jerold Simmons wrote: "The Wall is not just a sign that healing is taking place in the nation; it is the center of that healing."

Vietnam veteran and former Senator Bob Kerrey agrees. "It allowed people to understand loss, to value it, face it and grieve it, which is the hardest thing for human beings to do," he explained.

"This was something that gave Americans the license to mourn publicly," Scruggs said in a 2002 article in *USA Today*.

Baky concurs. "All of a sudden, it was alright to be associated with this event," he noted. "That's when all of the crying started in the presence of the monument."

"There's a difference between healing and catharsis," Scruggs said. Catharsis can be seen as a cleansing, a raw release of emotion; healing can be viewed as the repair or rebuilding of a broken spirit, an injured heart, a fractured society.

"For many veterans, The Wall offered a cathartic experience that helped," Scruggs explained.

While catharsis can be a step in the healing process, healing does not necessarily require catharsis. Scruggs remembered speaking with the actress Helen Hayes long after the dedication ceremonies for The Wall had taken place. She had watched reports of the ceremonies on television and recalled to Scruggs that she felt as if a burden had been lifted from her own shoulders.

That sense of relief was felt by many across the country and viewed as one of the initial signs that the nation was starting to heal. "It had a big impact almost immediately," Scruggs recalled.

Veteran and long-time volunteer Charlie Harootunian recalled his thoughts during the 1982 dedication ceremonies. "There were so many positive feelings," he said. "It [had been] very difficult to conceive what the Memorial was going to be like, what it was going to do. When we got there, all that controversy melted away."

Many of the veterans who attended the dedication ceremonies also found that when they returned home from their trips to Washington, D.C., they were greeted with flowers and notes from friends and colleagues. "It finally gave them the recognition that had been denied to them," said Scruggs.

But, healing is a long process. So while some of the healing could be felt almost immediately, much of it also needed to unfold slowly over time.

Dr. Donna Jackson, whose father, Robert G. Gerling, died Jan. 14, 1982 of complications stemming from Agent Orange exposure, believes that her healing did not really begin until she attended an *In Memory* ceremony at The Wall in 1996. "As I sat and listened to the speeches, I heard others put my thoughts and feelings into words. As they described their experiences,

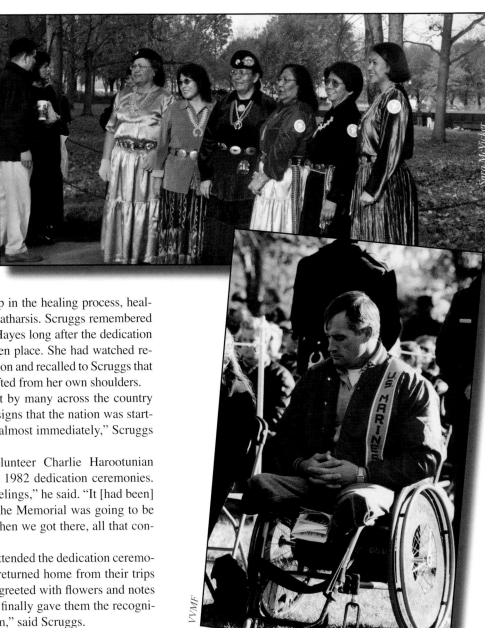

(Top) *Native American women veterans attend the 10th anniversary of the Vietnam Women's Memorial, November 2003.*

(Above) *A Marine veteran observes the ceremony on Veterans Day 1993.*

VVMF

Leroy Lawson

their emotions, their pain and confusion, I knew that I wasn't alone," she recalled. "I realized that they understood and, perhaps most important, that they cared."

While there, Jackson met a woman whose husband had died as a result of his service in Vietnam. "As we stood by The Wall and talked, I changed, and peace came," Jackson said. Sometimes healing arrived through the connections made at The Wall—through the hug, the arm put around a shoulder, the conversation with a kindred spirit.

Healing at The Wall occurs, Hass explained, "because none of the other memorials that have been built have the same kind of open quality. They're much more definitive about what it [the war] meant. [Whereas The Wall] doesn't come to any consensus, what it finds to agree on is the need to celebrate the sacrifice of the soldier, that's its great strength and that's why it heals so well."

Without question, the Memorial has had the ability to heal both the individuals who were suffering and a nation that was broken. Perhaps one of its greatest contributions to our country's healing has been in how it helped to shape our current perception and treatment of our nation's warriors. "During the Vietnam era," Scruggs explained, "we were not a supportive society. Today, you see a big difference with the men and women coming home from Iraq. While there's great disagreement about the war, there's great kindness, sympathy and support for the soldier. People can now separate the issue of the war and the people who are doing that duty."

(Previous page) Young people visit The Wall during a snowstorm.
(Inset) The crowds are undeterred by the snow on Veterans Day 1987.

(This page, above) An empty chair on stage with a helmet and boots symbolizes the POW/MIAs who cannot be present.

(Right) A mother and daughter grieve during the In Memory Ceremony 1996.

(Above) Families continue to leave remembrances for loved ones at The Wall.

(Right) Visitors gather at The Wall on Veterans Day 1984.

OFFERINGS AT THE WALL

One of the most unique aspects of the public's interaction with the Memorial is its practice of leaving objects at The Wall. These items are tangible, personal mementos brimming with meaning—not merely the flowers or wreaths traditionally left at a gravesite.

Numerous questions arise each time an object is left. Who is it for? What does it represent? Why did the person feel the need to part with the item? Why part with it now?

While the answers are largely unknown, one fact is certain: the practice of leaving items began at The Wall and forever changed how we show our public support to those suffering through tragedy and to those who have died.

When people started to leave items at The Wall, Pam West, director of the Museum Resource Center (MRCE) in Landover, Md., was unsure what to do with them. "We searched high and low to see if there was any type of collection anywhere else out there like it," she remembered. They were unable to find any.

"I looked at this box of items that this maintenance worker had collected. I looked at this teddy bear and thought 'I don't know if I could have left my son's teddy bear at The Wall,'" West recalled.

"The Vietnam collection is the first of its type," she continued. "It was the first time that things that should have been handed down generation to generation weren't. When you look at the medals, things that should have been handed down to a grandson, for me, it was a no-brainer [to collect the items]." West and her staff began to archive the items convinced that they held value, purpose and meaning.

"The surprising part for everybody was people's tendency to leave things. Nobody had really thought of that occurring," said Scruggs. "It's provided a great legacy for the Memorial and for American society."

But how or why did that legacy begin? In her book, Hass theorized that the "absence of a clearly stated government position on the war in the design of the Memorial tacitly asked people to respond to the Memorial with their own interpretations." This, combined with the individual names, the Memorial's ability to reflect images, evolving funerary practices and shifting cultural values, all contributed to the phenomenon of offering objects at The Wall, she explained.

"People have responded to the individuated memory that The Wall makes with a new memorial impulse. Leaving something at The Wall is an act of negotiating each of these relationships, between the dead and the nation, the dead and the past, and the dead and the living—in the face of a changing social and political universe," Hass wrote.

Bill Petros

Visitors share a moment of remembering during the Veterans Day Ceremony 2006.

Stuffed animals are a popular item to leave at The Wall.

Terry Adams, National Park Service

"Leaving things is the invitation to the culture to participate in grieving," Baky explained. In addition to the public tears, the items left behind serve as a tangible sign that we have connected to The Wall and to each other in the grieving and healing process.

Percoco noted that our changed society also played a large role in these far more public displays of grief. "We're in the age of full disclosure. We're a much more public culture," he said. "We're used to airing grievances in public. People beforehand didn't have that same sort of sentiment. Death was a much more private thing."

In essence, we now invite others to be spectators in our shared pain. "The personal artifacts that have been left at the Memorial—photographs, letters, teddy bears, MIA/POW bracelets, clothes, medals of honor—are offered up as testimony, transposed from personal to cultural artifacts, to bear witness to pain suffered," Sturken wrote.

It's not an accident that this phenomenon happens at The Wall, Baky reasoned. The Wall was created by the veterans themselves and paid for by the public. "You couldn't leave a teddy bear if the government had created the Memorial," he said.

While the practice began at The Wall, it has now become a common occurrence in response to a variety of situations. When a child is murdered on a street corner, an impromptu shrine of teddy bears, notes and trinkets will arise. On highway after highway, mini memorials are erected at the sites of fatal accidents.

In Oklahoma City following the bombing, a chain link fence was erected around the bombing site. There, stuffed into the gaps between or tied to the fence links, people left plush toys, cards, letters, medals, ribbons, T-shirts, American flags, key chains and silk flowers.

Our reaction to celebrity deaths has also changed. The outpouring of items left behind for Princess Diana stretched for miles along the funeral procession route, at several palaces and at the island where her body was laid to rest. The entrance to the apartment building where John F. Kennedy Jr. lived at the time of his death was adorned with cards, mementos, flowers and photos. Contrast that to the public reaction following the death of John Lennon, which occurred Dec. 8, 1980—just two years prior to the building of The Wall. After Lennon's death, there were groups of people who congregated, sang and held lit candles, but few placed items on the sidewalk where he was shot. If his death were to occur today, that would certainly not be the case. Instead, it is more likely that an extravagant display

Many different items are left at The Wall. The insignia on the small remembrance cards in the background is that of the 199th Light Infantry Brigade, the unit Jan Scruggs served in.

Terry Adams, National Park Service

(This page and the opposite page) Schoolchildren look at items left at The Wall.

Leroy Lawson

Leroy Lawson

(This page and opposite page) Every item left at The Wall has meaning.

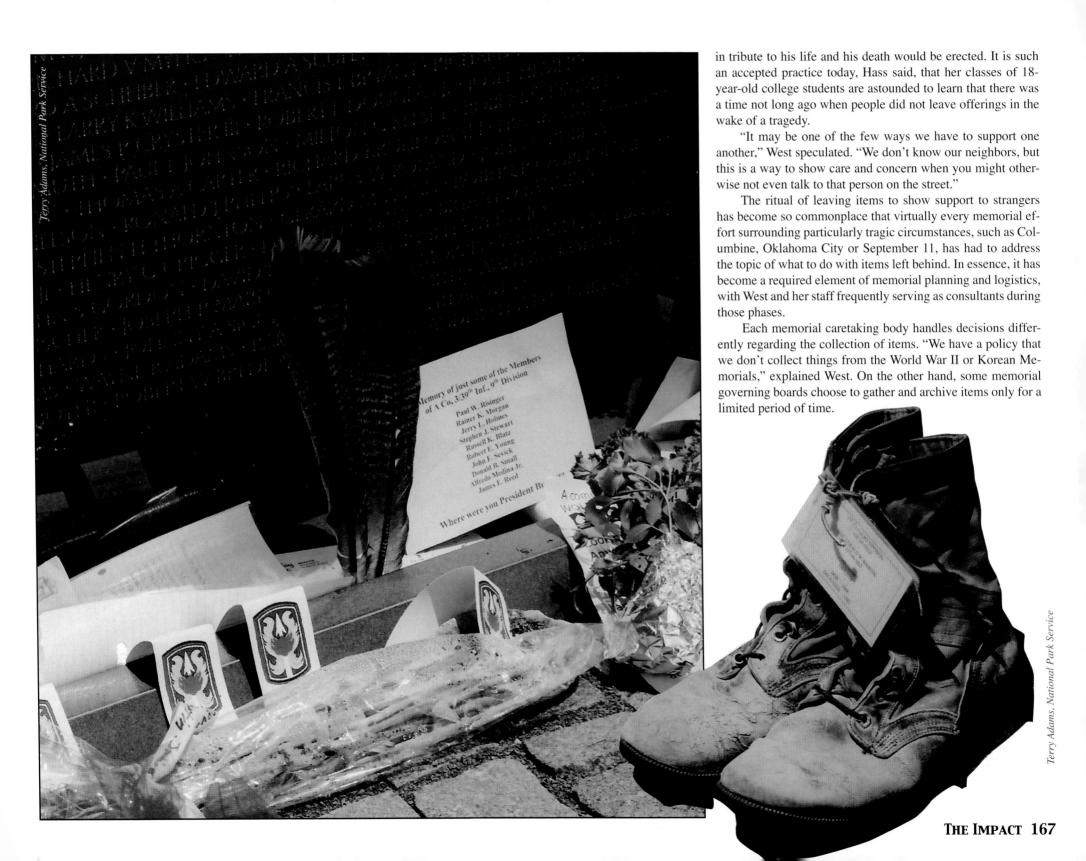

in tribute to his life and his death would be erected. It is such an accepted practice today, Hass said, that her classes of 18-year-old college students are astounded to learn that there was a time not long ago when people did not leave offerings in the wake of a tragedy.

"It may be one of the few ways we have to support one another," West speculated. "We don't know our neighbors, but this is a way to show care and concern when you might otherwise not even talk to that person on the street."

The ritual of leaving items to show support to strangers has become so commonplace that virtually every memorial effort surrounding particularly tragic circumstances, such as Columbine, Oklahoma City or September 11, has had to address the topic of what to do with items left behind. In essence, it has become a required element of memorial planning and logistics, with West and her staff frequently serving as consultants during those phases.

Each memorial caretaking body handles decisions differently regarding the collection of items. "We have a policy that we don't collect things from the World War II or Korean Memorials," explained West. On the other hand, some memorial governing boards choose to gather and archive items only for a limited period of time.

Memory of just some of the Members
of A Co, 3/39ᵗʰ Inf., 9ᵗʰ Division

Paul W. Risinger
Rainer K. Morgan
Jerry L. Holmes
Stephen J. Stewart
Russell K. Blatz
Robert E. Young
John F. Sevick
Donald B. Small
Alfredo Medina Jr.
James E. Reed

Where were you President Br

Terry Adams, National Park Service

As for the Vietnam Veterans Memorial, the MRCE sees no end in sight in terms of collecting items. There are still hundreds of items left at The Wall each month, even now, 25 years after its dedication. "The time release concept comes from the [idea] that you have to release yourself from the nightmares to be able to come to The Wall," explained Harry Robinson during the March 26, 2007 panel on the changing face of the National Mall. "There's [also] a certain time-release factor during which someone is ready to let go and leave something at The Wall, and is willing to let go of that memory in dispensable form and submit it to the power of The Wall."

In West's opinion, "there are still so many vets who haven't gone to The Wall. It's not time yet to stop collecting the items. There are too many people who still have to come and leave things."

Bill Petros

Many of the items left at The Wall have a patriotic theme.

Bill Petros

VVMF © Frederick E. Hart/VVMF, 1984

A family relaxes together during the Memorial Day Ceremony 2007.

(Left) There are always offerings at The Wall. (Above) The Three Servicemen stand, ever vigilant.

John Jr · EAL Donnelly

The Spirit of the Wall

RICHARD D YARKER · JAMES B RO
HAROLD E BURKETT · ROBERT D DON
NNETH D GILMORE · ROBERT F GUTH
OHN A JOHNSON · MARVIN L LINDLE
WARD E PHILLIPS · JOHN M QUINN · J
THOMAS Jr · TERRY LEE WELLER · GEN
R P AUGUSTINAS · GEORGE A BROWN
FORRESTER · BILLY G FRY · JOHN H GR
LLIAM T HAYNES · GALEN F HUMPHRE
SELL B LUKER · THOMAS E McGRAW · A
PETER G VLAHAKOS · DOUGLAS M WE
N I CAMERON · JOHN R DUSBABEK · S
GERALD C LYMAN · DENNIS M O'NEILL
AMES L CARTER + WILLIAM M COOMES
EDWARD M PARSLEY · ARD C STE
A-VILLAFANE · W LLIA III · RC

Boots are often left at The Wall.

170

SON · GLENN F DRAKE ·
EUGENE D HAMILTON ·
UGENE T McCOY ·
H A RANDAZZO ·
WILLIAMS ·
LLARD R BURNLEY ·
H · JERRY RAY RAMBERGER ·
ILLIAM JONES ·
T M PREVOST ·
RE · MICHAEL I SHANER ·
J ELYEA · RICHARD SMITH ·
HARD G PHILBIN ·
HARD C YOUNGBEAR ·
T · THERMAN
D L BE

Daniel Arant

Terry Adams, National Park Service

171

Bill Petros

THE WALL AS AN ICON

Collective memory, a term first coined by Maurice Halbwachs, a French philosopher and sociologist, refers to the shared memory of a group or society, separating it from the concept of individual memory. What we choose to memorialize, and what we choose not to memorialize, are indicators of the collective memory. Consequently, our history and how we recall it is shaped by the very memorials we choose to erect.

"History, and how the public knows of it, gets distilled and frozen in iconic objects like The Wall," explained Baky. "Popular perception of historical events somehow needs to be rendered into an icon that people can tuck away and [when] they see that, it stands for myriad other things. It's what symbols are; it's the importance of mythology and how myths work."

It did not take long for The Wall to be embraced as an icon. Likely contributing to its rapid acceptance was the fact that its image had been broadcast into our own homes. The groundbreaking, as well as the dedication of both The Wall and the Three Servicemen statue, received national media coverage.

According to Percoco, we are also eager to embrace our monuments and memorials. They speak to our values and our sense of patriotism. "As a nation, we practice 'civic religion.' We've created these memorials as temples to worship at," said Percoco. "We practice iconography that's not tied to a religious faith, but we certainly practice it in this country."

As The Wall secured iconic status, it facilitated its own reinvention, as Baky described. That reinventing, or re-remembering, is what accounts for the shifting historical narrative surrounding the Vietnam War.

Baky provided an example of the evolving narrative that has resulted, "At first, the war was universally bad. Then in the 1990s and 2000s, it moved 180 degrees, with the notion of the veteran as hero or unsuspecting victim that supplants the notion of the bad war," he said.

For veterans, it can be difficult to see the shift. "They [often] don't see how dramatic the change has been in that perception," Baky added. "What they remember is what's painful, the fact that they were ignored. In terms of the valorization of the veteran, which came later, they don't really buy that [concept] in the absence of seeing example after example." But there are hundreds, if not thousands, of examples in pop culture of the use of The Wall as an icon and the veteran as a heroic figure.

Bill Petros

(Above) Dignitaries who attended the groundbreaking 25 years ago gather again for the anniversary ceremony on March 26, 2007. From left: Sen. Chuck Hagel (R-Neb.); former Sen. Charles Mathias (R-Md.); Sen. John Warner (R-Va.); and Jan Scruggs, Memorial Fund.

(Left) Gold Star Mothers attend the Memorial Day Ceremony 2007.

Leroy Lawson

A young boy reads a letter left at The Wall.

Daniel Avant

INFLUENCING POP CULTURE

Scholars, historians, veterans and artists all agree that the Vietnam Veterans Memorial opened up communication about the war and the events surrounding it. While it was no longer a taboo subject, the controversies did not disappear; rather, people were free to explore and process all of their perceptions in their many permutations. The result was a surge in the materials that are an expression of pop culture: books, movies, songs, comics, memorabilia and nostalgic items with a focus on the Vietnam War or on The Wall.

"What the public 'knows' is not by reading historical accounts, not by digesting historical text," Baky observed. "As it turns out, how the public knows historical events is through popular culture."

One example, he noted, is how many hundreds of thousands of people worldwide have seen the musical "Miss Saigon," a modern adaptation of "Madame Butterfly," which tells the story of a Vietnamese woman abandoned by her American Marine lover during the fall of Saigon. "Try to find a textbook that has sold more than a few thousand copies," explained Baky, with the point being that our perceptions are shaped by these far more pervasive and accessible materials.

And of course, there is television's impact. "There have been 47 TV series, like 'Matt Houston' and 'Magnum, P.I.,' that have three or more episodes about the Vietnam War, just in the past 20 years," Baky described. "Again, compare the number of people who have seen 'Magnum, P.I.' vs. the number who have read a particular text book."

The Connelly Library at La Salle University, where Baky is director, is home to one of the largest, most unique collections of pop culture items related to the Vietnam War era. In addition to being an expert in this area, Baky is also a Vietnam veteran.

"People want to reject how fiction handles issues. It's not an accident that fiction has been thought of as the lie that speaks truth," said Baky. "It's very hard to talk about experience when you're just using data. In a way, data trivializes it. It's too cold, whereas novels, films, short stories and poetry are much better at synthesizing it for us."

"Watching anything painful or even when reading novels, your perception increases exponentially. You start to think about *how* you're thinking about things," he explained. "That's what also happens in films about war. You hear a lot of criticism about them, but that's because there are a lot of bad films. But the good ones reveal things in really good ways. So, if you get one good film, it's worth the hundreds of bad ones."

Baky documented that the number of commercial films and novels released after The Wall increased dramatically. When The Wall was dedicated in 1982, there was essentially a handful in existence. But by 1986 and into the early 1990s, there were hundreds on the market. "When a publisher decides they're going to put money behind something, you know things have changed," Baky noted.

Many artists, authors and producers, such as Lionel Chetwynd, also felt a noticeable shift in perceptions. Chetwynd wrote the motion picture screenplay adaptation for "The Apprenticeship of Duddy Kravitz" and received an Academy Award nomination and the Writers Guild of America Award for Best Feature Comedy. He also has over 40 feature and long-form television credits, including the Vietnam trilogy: "The Hanoi Hilton," "To Heal a Nation" and "Kissinger and Nixon." "To Heal a Nation" is the story of Scruggs' effort to build the Memorial.

(Previous page) Visitors can see their own reflections on The Wall.

(This page) Crowds come even when it rains.

When Chetwynd first arrived in Hollywood, he noticed that it portrayed Vietnam vets merely as one-dimensional characters. "There was a time before The Wall when a script would say, 'Charlie walks into the room, scruffy, with a bandana around his head, typical Vietnam vet type.' Hollywood tends to think in stereotypes. That was the view of vets then," Chetwynd recalled.

So, while veterans could occasionally be portrayed on television or on film, it was only within the confines of the stereotype. "What The Wall did," Chetwynd explained, "was put a human face on the veterans. Suddenly, these were people being reflected back, the names were human, and it freed me from paying homage to the stereotype."

Still, according to Chetwynd, relatively few people in Hollywood had actually served in the military. As a result, many of the works had an anti-war sentiment—although they made great progress in portraying those who served and making them rich, multi-dimensional characters. "In popular culture, there was a humanizing of the veterans with 'Full Metal Jacket,' 'Born on the Fourth of July' and 'Platoon,'" Chetwynd explained. All three movies were released between 1986 and 1989.

As The Wall gained iconic status, Hollywood frequently adopted it in order to make a statement. "Then everyone wanted to have a scene at The Wall," Chetwynd remembered. "The Wall became a visual cue to the audience. It gave substance to the claim that 'this movie is about the warrior and not the war.'"

The film industry wasn't the only one to adopt The Wall in order to send a specific message. "I've got a notebook 13 inches thick with nothing but advertisements of products that incorporate the use of The Wall or some part of The Wall in the ad," Baky explained. Many of the ads involve legitimate use of The Wall in support of related fundraising efforts. But, many more commandeered the image for completely unrelated causes and products.

Another result of the Memorial as a pop culture icon is that it spawned the growth of a nostalgia industry. "Numerous

magazines that re-examine and recount Vietnam War experiences have emerged; the merchandizing of Frederick Hart's statue (which include posters, T-shirts, a Franklin Mint miniature and a plastic model kit)," Sturken wrote. Some banks even offered customers the option of having The Wall's image imprinted on checks.

One of the more significant iconic depictions of The Wall was its use on a U.S. Postal Service commemorative postage stamp. It has been featured twice: first in 1984, just two years after its dedication. Then in 2000, it was selected by the public during a nationwide balloting on the Internet to be included as one of 15 commemoratives saluting the 1980s. Other 1980s commemoratives that were part of the "Celebrate the Century" series included the fall of the Berlin Wall, the hostages coming home, cable television, the space shuttle program, the musical "Cats," personal computers and Cabbage Patch Kids. Not only did The Wall work to reshape our interpretation of the war, it became symbolic of an entirely separate decade: the one in which it was born.

In the literary world, you could also see the changing perception of the war reflected. Most compelling was the evolution of the cover art that appeared on paperbacks, poetry books and videotapes. "You literally can track the perception of the war as we remember it, using reissues of the same book," Baky said. "You're not changing the actual story; you're changing the visual of what the public is seeing on the book rack."

In essence, the selected artwork reflects the publisher's decision regarding what it believes the public will embrace in terms of the story. "If you look across a decade, it's fascinating," he said. "I must have at least 16 or 17 examples of cover art changing. You don't realize it unless you see all of them together."

According to Chetwynd, "One of the lessons of Jan's journey in 'To Heal a Nation' is that those who serve should not leave it to the popular culture to tell their story. In every case, they should use their resources to see that it is justly told."

Vietnam Veterans Memorial Stamp © 1984, United States Postal Service. All Rights Reserved. Used with permission.

POW/MIA Stamp © 1995, United States Postal Service. All Rights Reserved. Used with permission.

Vietnam Veterans Memorial Hand on The Wall Stamp © 2000, United States Postal Service. All Rights Reserved. Used with permission.

(Previous page, top left) Sen. John Warner (R-Va.) has been a constant supporter of the Memorial over the years. (Bottom left) Edward L. Times, Co. B, 1/7 Cav., salutes at The Wall after laying a wreath. He has been laying the wreath for the 1st Cavalry since 1995. (Bottom right) A color guard stands at the apex during a ceremony.

(This page, from top) A stamp commemorating the Vietnam Veterans Memorial was issued November 10, 1984. (Center) A large image of the POW/MIA stamp was placed atop The Wall for the Memorial Day Ceremony in 1995. (Bottom) A stamp declaring The Wall as one of the icons of the 1980s is unveiled in January 2000. Jan Scruggs (second from left) and American Gold Star Mothers attend the unveiling.

Bill Gray

VVM

The Wall is attracts visitors at night, as well as during the day.

The crowds at the Veterans Day ceremony in 1984 for the dedication
of the Three Servicemen statue were especially large.

Its Changing Role over Time

"If Jan Scruggs had been in the Korean War and tried in the mid-1950s to create this, he couldn't have made this happen," explained Harry Robinson during the March 26 panel discussion about The Wall's impact on the National Mall. "Because the cultural attitude in this country hadn't turned to the understanding of the work of the masses." So timing, changing values and the nation's intense desire to reconcile its past all played a role in bringing about the Memorial.

Now, as Scruggs has noted, "Wherever you go — Beijing, Dublin, Berlin, Mexico City — the Vietnam Veterans Memorial, or 'The Wall,' is an instantly recognizable symbol of America. That says a lot about how important this Memorial is to our culture."

And it is still equally — or even more — important to the individual veterans and family members who continue to visit again and again. "One of the things I've come to know about The Wall is that no matter how many times you go there, it's different every time; the story is never finished," explained Robinson. "One day, you go there, and you're thinking about this set of events; the next time, it's another set of events. Each time you go, you learn and relearn."

Joe Galloway, co-author of *We Were Soldiers Once… and Young* and a pre-eminent war correspondent who spent four tours in Vietnam, explained that in many ways visiting The Wall has grown increasingly difficult through the years. "It doesn't get easier; it gets harder," he said, "because back then, all of us were young. We didn't really know all of the things that they gave up. Now we do. We've known the joy of loving a good wife, being a father, raising children and seeing them successful. All of that makes their sacrifice only more deeply felt."

But what will the Memorial mean 50 to 100 years from now after the Vietnam generation has passed? Regardless of what historians and scholars eventually conclude, Scruggs sees the Memorial's greatest legacy as its ability to heal, to educate and to save lives. "Many good things have come from this Memorial: in people's lives; in that it will always be considered a great work of American architecture; in that it is recognized as a history lesson for the country; and that we've been able to expand that opportunity to save lives in Vietnam, especially lives of young farm kids. The Memorial will stand the test of time," said Scruggs.

While the long list of accomplishments could never have been predicted, Scruggs understood his initial vision required a gamble. "There is a risk-reward model in life," he explained. "Sometimes with the risks we take in life, there are great rewards."

Great rewards did follow the risks taken by Scruggs and the Memorial Fund; rewards that will benefit generations to come.

(Above) A rainstorm will not deter visitors attending ceremonies at The Wall.

(Left) Many of the visitors to The Wall each year are children.

A group from the 24th Evacuation Hospital visits the nation's capital on Veterans Day 2002.

(Above) Sen. Chuck Hagel (R-Neb.) addresses the crowds on Veterans Day.

(Left) A visitor makes a name rubbing.

APPENDIX 1

VIETNAM VETERANS MEMORIAL FUND BOARD OF DIRECTORS

Founder and President
Jan C. Scruggs
Vietnam Veterans Memorial Fund
Washington, D.C.

Chairman of the Board
John O. Woods
Woods Peacock Engineering Consultants Inc.
Alexandria, Va.

Treasurer
Robert H. Frank
Frank & Company, pc
McLean, Va.

Directors
John Dibble
Attorney at Law
Washington, D.C.

James V. Kimsey
The Kimsey Foundation
Washington, D.C.

George W. Mayo Jr., Esq.
Hogan & Hartson L.L.P.
Washington, D.C.

Lt. Col. Janis Nark, USAR (Ret.)
Aspen, Colo.

Harry G. Robinson III, FAIA
TRG International
Washington, D.C.

Leroy Lawson

Many wreaths are laid at The Wall during the Veterans Day Ceremony.

(Above and left) National Park Service personnel and volunteers wash The Wall every weekend between April and November.

APPENDIX 2

VIETNAM VETERANS MEMORIAL FUND STAFF

Jan C. Scruggs
Founder and President

Holly Rotondi
Vice President of Programs

Sara Foxx
Office Manager

Lisa Gough
Director of Communications

Mariah Payne
Director of Education

Jessica Perno
Program Associate

JoAnn Waller
Assistant to the President

Geoff Wiles
Development Associate

Chuck Searcy
In-Country Representative
Project RENEW™

Barbara Smith
Cary Dees
Site Managers
The Wall That Heals

Park service personnel, organizations and families all volunteer their time to wash The Wall.

Appendix 3

Vietnam Veterans Memorial Volunteers

Terry E. Brown
Volunteer Liaison
National Park Service

Alaska
Nancy Smoyer

California
Terry Martens
Donna Prince

Colorado
Suzanne Sigona

Delaware
Joseph D. Goss

District of Columbia
Annmarie Emmet
Bobby Jackson
Leroy Lawson
Robert E. Marshall
Pete and Tamora Papas
O'Donald Parker
Paul J. Rozek

Florida
Bobbie Keith
Jim and Marcia Stepanek

Illinois
Paul A. Baffico

Indiana
Richard Barrett

Kentucky
Barbara Johnson

Maryland
Lee Adriani

Daniel R. Arant
Robert J. Campbell
Gene and Nancy Cliff
Lynn Clinedinst
Mary Jane Gerity
Joseph Goss
James A. Hontz Jr.
Robert Harkins
Gary Johnson
Patricia Liegey
Allen McCabe
William Struck
Glenn E. Watkins
Paddy Wiesenfeld, Ph.D.

Massachusetts
Charlie Harootunian
Ginni Porter

Missouri
Paula Allison
Ron Stufflebean

North Carolina
Donna R. Bartlett

New Jersey
Michael Coale
Ann Kelsey
Joseph Leone
Michael G. McMahon
Benjamin Peters

New York
Jim Schueckler

Ohio
Cindy Smith
Alan Wallace

Oregon
Roger C. King

Pennsylvania
Susan Coleman Fowler
Kelly Coleman Rihn
John C. Devlin
Arthur Drescher
Ron Edgington
S. Red Flegal
James Goss
Edward Leskin
The Rev. John C. Obenchain
Frank Richardson
Paul and Cyndy Stancliff
Larry R. Walters II
Ron Worstell

Tennessee
Regina Talley

Texas
Mack Easley

Virginia
Gary O. Alton
Mardy Bosch
Bill and Fran Chester
Richard W. Daley
Anthony Fasolo
Sidney L. George
Lynne Gomez
Emmelene Gura
William Harris
Elizabeth Henry
Earl J. Hovermill
Faye Hull
Richard A. Huxta
Dan Kirby
Beth Lawrence
Marney Michalowski
Philip K. Scruggs
Tom Tabor
Kelly Wenner

Daniel Arant © Frederick E. Hart/VVMF, 1984

A young visitor braves the cold to visit The Wall.

Leroy Lawson

APPENDIX 4

CONTACT THE MEMORIAL FUND

For information on any of the Memorial Fund's activities or programs, contact:
Vietnam Veterans Memorial Fund
1023 Fifteenth St., NW
Second Floor
Washington, DC 20005
Phone: (202) 393-0090
Fax: (202) 393-0029
E-mail: *vvmf@vvmf.org*
Web site: *www.vvmf.org*

DIRECTORY OF NAMES

(From Chapter 3)
The Vietnam Veterans Memorial *Directory of Names* can be purchased by contacting:
Guest Services Inc.
3055 Prosperity Ave.
Fairfax, VA 20031
(703) 849-9300

Tom Estrin

Veterans often come to The Wall with the comrades they served with to remember the friends they lost.

ADDING A NAME TO THE WALL

(From Chapter 3)

The Vietnam Veterans Memorial Fund does not make the decisions about which names are added to The Wall. These decisions are made by the Department of Defense. The Memorial Fund does not have the authority to overrule those who adjudicate these matters.

For further explanation of the parameters for inclusion, please contact the relevant service branch:

Army
Mortuary Affairs and Casualty Support
2461 Eisenhower Ave.
Alexandria, VA 22331-0482
Fax: (703) 325-5315

Air Force
Headquarters Air Force Personnel Center
Missing Persons Branch
550 C. St. West, Suite 14
Randolph AFB, TX 78150-4716
Fax: (210) 565-3805

Marine
Headquarters U.S. Marine Corps
Manpower and Reserve Affairs, MRC
3280 Russell Rd.
Quantico, VA 22134-5103
Fax: (703) 784-9823

Navy
Navy Personnel Command
Casualty Assistance Branch (PERS-621P
5720 Integrity Dr.
Millington, TN 38055-6210
Fax: (901) 874-6654

Daniel Arant

Visitors come to The Wall to remember, pay tribute and show respect for fallen comrades. Here, a veteran salutes his brothers in arms.

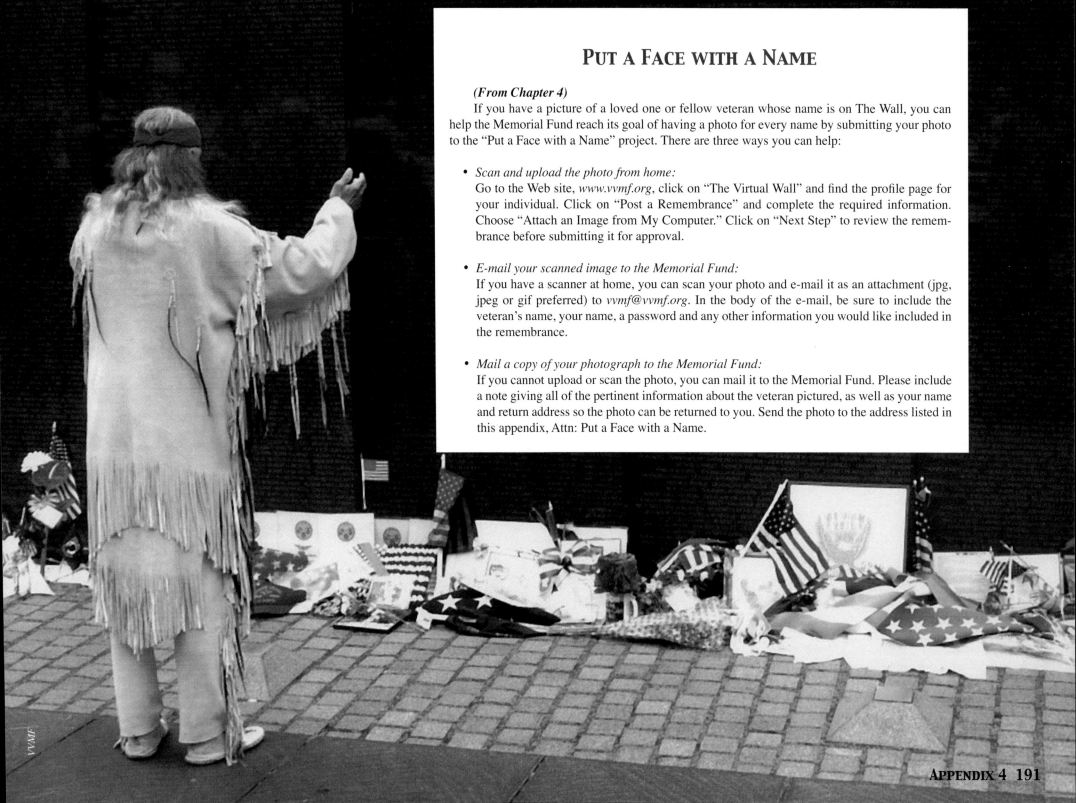

PUT A FACE WITH A NAME

(From Chapter 4)

    If you have a picture of a loved one or fellow veteran whose name is on The Wall, you can help the Memorial Fund reach its goal of having a photo for every name by submitting your photo to the "Put a Face with a Name" project. There are three ways you can help:

- *Scan and upload the photo from home:*
  Go to the Web site, *www.vvmf.org*, click on "The Virtual Wall" and find the profile page for your individual. Click on "Post a Remembrance" and complete the required information. Choose "Attach an Image from My Computer." Click on "Next Step" to review the remembrance before submitting it for approval.

- *E-mail your scanned image to the Memorial Fund:*
  If you have a scanner at home, you can scan your photo and e-mail it as an attachment (jpg, jpeg or gif preferred) to *vvmf@vvmf.org*. In the body of the e-mail, be sure to include the veteran's name, your name, a password and any other information you would like included in the remembrance.

- *Mail a copy of your photograph to the Memorial Fund:*
  If you cannot upload or scan the photo, you can mail it to the Memorial Fund. Please include a note giving all of the pertinent information about the veteran pictured, as well as your name and return address so the photo can be returned to you. Send the photo to the address listed in this appendix, Attn: Put a Face with a Name.

Name rubbings are a valuable way for visitors to take a reminder of their Wall visit home with them.

REQUEST A NAME RUBBING

(From Chapter 5)

If you cannot visit The Wall, volunteers will make a rubbing of a name and send it to you. To receive a free name rubbing, contact the Memorial

Leroy Lawson

Volunteers Red Flegal (left) and Tom Tabor (right) make name rubbings for visitors at The Wall.

BECOME A VOLUNTEER

(From Chapter 5)

There are a number of ways to become a volunteer at the Vietnam Veterans Memorial. One is by registering with the National Park Service (NPS). Contact the Vietnam Veterans Memorial NPS kiosk at (202) 634-1568 or (202) 426-6843.

Volunteers may also sign up with the Vietnam Veterans Memorial Fund. The Memorial Fund engages in a number of commemorative and educational activities aimed at preserving the legacy of the Vietnam Veterans Memorial, promoting healing and educating about the impact of the Vietnam War. Long-distance volunteers can assist visitors at the Memorial Fund's *The Wall That Heals* Traveling Memorial and Museum. Contact the Memorial Fund at (202) 393-0090 or via e-mail at *vvmf@vvmf.org*.

VVMF

Leroy Lawson

The Color Guard folds the flag, Veterans Day 1993.

Women who served in Vietnam visit the nation's capital.

The Jewish War Veterans lay a wreath, Veterans Day 1993.

Bagpiper Walter Wilke salutes while the bugler plays Taps, Veterans Day 1997.

Winter is a beautiful time at The Wall.

Daniel Arant

Another young visitor discovers The Wall.

Tom Estrin

Members of the Vietnam Helicopter Pilots Association and the Veterans of Foreign Wars place their wreaths at The Wall.

Brig. Gen. George Price, USA, attends the snowy Veterans Day Ceremony in 1987.

A sailor has his re-enlistment ceremony at The Wall.

Families come to The Wall to remember loved ones.

Flags, flowers and medals are some of the many
items people leave at The Wall to pay tribute.

The White House

Sen. Jay Rockefeller (D-W.Va.) applauds as President Bill Clinton is introduced by Gen. Colin Powell, Memorial Day 1993.

Sen. John Warner (R-Va.), Sen. Chuck Hagel (R-Neb.), American Gold Star Mothers President Betty Pulliam, Gold Star Mother Ann Wolcott and Brig. Gen. George Price, USA (Ret.) attend the ceremony blessing the site of the Memorial Center.

Daniel Arant

Visitors of all ages come to The Wall
and leave all sorts of items in tribute.

Leroy Lawson

Amelia Arria

203

Sunrise at The Wall is always beautiful.

Daniel Arant

INDEX

A

Adams, Terry 6
Adriani, Lee 107, 109, 110, 111, 112, 115, 124, 125, 185
Alabama 79, 84
Allison, Paula 185
Alton, Gary O. 185
Anderson, Kurt 33
Anderson, Linda 6
Arant, Dan 6, 112, 114, 185
Arria, Amelia 6

B

Baffico, Paul A. 185
Baky, John 149, 155 157, 172, 175, 177
Bannion, Jim 6
Barrett, Rick 117, 185
Bartlett, Donna R. 185
Belluschi, Pietro 20, 21
Bever, Lt. Cmdr. Jerry 15
Bonior, Rep. David 93
Bosch, Frank 110, 124
Bosch, Mardy 185
Brewer, Scott 25
Brown, Jesse 78
Brown, Terry E. 185
Broyles, William 55
Bumpers, Sen. Dale 15
Burr, Andrus "Andy" 23
Bush, Barbara 142
Bush, President George H.W. 93, 142, 157
Bush, President George W. 142

C

Campbell, Robert 23
Campbell, Robert J. 185
Carhart, Tom 15, 25
Carter, President Jimmy 17
Carter, Rosalynn 17
Century, Larry 45
Chester, Bill 185
Chester, Fran 185
Chetwynd, Lionel 175, 177
Choquette, Bill 24
Clark, Jane 30
Clark, Interior Secretary William P. 30
Clay, Grady 20, 21, 23
Cleland, Sen. Max 93
Cliff, Gene 185
Cliff, Nancy 185
Clinedinst, Lynn 185
Clinton, President Bill 78, 79, 202
Coale, Michael 116, 117, 185
Coleman, Joel D. 95
Cooper, Kent 24, 25
Copulos, Milt 29
Cotsakos, Christos M. 95
Crew, Spencer R. 155
Cummings, James "J.C." 38, 46, 49, 50, 55, 107
Cupp, Emogene 16, 45, 154
Cupp, Robert 16

D

Daley, Richard W. 118, 185
Davison, Gen. Mike 27
Dees, Cary 183
Deutsch, Master Sgt. Jonathan 66
Devlin, John C. 185
Dibble, John 181
Dole, Sen. Robert 15, 93, 157
Doubek, Bob 13, 14, 15, 16, 17, 19, 23, 24, 25, 29, 33, 45, 58
Downs, Brig. Gen. Michael 61
Drescher, Arthur 51, 109, 185
Drescher, Barbara 51
Drescher, Bonnie 51

E

Easley, Mack 185
Eckbo, Garrett 20
Edgington, Ron 40, 115, 117, 185
Emmet, Annmarie 62, 107, 111, 112, 119, 185
Estrin, Tom 6
Evans, Diane Carlson 39

F

Fasolo, Anthony 108, 185
Fauriol, Sandie 25
Felton, Duery 129, 131, 133, 135, 137
Flegal, Stephen "Red" 109, 111, 117, 119, 124, 185, 194
Ford, President Gerald 17, 93, 137

Fowler, Susan Coleman 185
Foxx, Sara 183
Frank, Bob 14, 20, 181
French, Heather Renee 79
Freud, Sigmund 13

G

Galloway, Joe 74, 84, 179
George, Sid 109, 117, 124, 185
Gerity, Mary Jane 185
Gerling, Robert G. 79, 157
Gibbs, Ron 15
Gomez, Lynne 185
Goodacre, Glenna 39
Goss, James 185
Goss, Joseph 185
Gough, Lisa 6, 183
Graves, Danny 92
Gray, Bill 6
Greenwood, Lee 79
Gura, Emmelene 106, 119, 185

H

Haaga, Paul 14
Hagel, Sen. Chuck 27, 79, 93, 172, 180, 202
Halbwachs, Maurice 172
Harkins, Robert 185
Harootunian, Charlie 65, 107, 109, 111, 113, 117, 119, 121, 124, 125, 157, 185
Harris, Emmy Lou 79

Harris, William 185
Hart, Frederick 29, 30, 31
Harter, Bill 40
Hass, Kristin 129, 145, 147, 152, 159, 160
Hatch, Elizabeth "Libby" Denison 71, 109, 124
Hattemer, Henry 152
Hayes, Helen 157
Healy, Monica 6, 15, 16, 17, 25, 27
Henry, Betty 107, 185
Herd, Ann 154
Hontz, James A. Jr. 185
Hope, Bob 17, 78, 79
Hovermill, Earl J. 185
Hull, Faye 185
Hunt, Richard 20
Huxta, Richard A. 185

J

Jackson, Bobby 185
Jackson, Donna 79, 157, 159
Jayne, Bill 15, 29
Johnson, Barbara 118, 185
Johnson, Gary 185
Joyce, Kevin 113
Judd, Naomi 78
Judd, Wynonna 78
Jung, Carl 13

K

Keith, Bobbie 185

INDEX

Kelsey, Ann 185
Kerrey, Sen. Bob 157
Kerry, Sen. John 78, 79
Kiefer, Alena L. 4
Kimsey, James V. 181
King, Andrew 147, 152
King, Rev. Martin Luther 27
King, Roger C. 185
Kingsley, James 45
Kirby, Dan 185
Koppel, Ted 79
Kuralt, Charles 33

L

Lamb, Lia 75
Lawrence, Beth 185
Lawson, Leroy 6, 48, 111, 185
Lecky, Bill 6, 24, 25, 29, 43, 46
Leone, Joseph 185
Leskin, Edward 6, 185
Liegey, Patricia 185
Lin, Maya 6, 21, 23, 24, 25, 27, 29, 38, 43, 45, 55, 57, 93, 145, 147
Luebke, Thomas 147, 149

M

MacDonald, Country Joe 79
Markey, Rep. Edward 61
Marquart, John 24
Marr, Bill 14, 15
Marshall, Robert E. 185
Martens, Terry 185

Mathias, Sen. Charles "Mac" 8, 15, 16, 17, 27, 172
Mayo, George W. "Sandy" 14, 20, 77, 181
McCabe, Allen 111, 185
McCaffrey, Gen. Barry R. 78, 93
McCann, Murray 15
McDermott, John 79
McGar, Brian Kent 51
McGovern, George 13
McKenzie, Scott 79
McMahon, Michael G. 185
McVicker, Sara 6
Michalowski, Marney 185
Moore, Gen. Hal 84
Morrison, John 14
Morrissey, Tom 6
Mosley, Art 14, 15, 19, 29
Mudd, Roger 14
Murphy, Kim 1, 6
Murtha, Rep. John 45
Myers, Gen. Richard 79

N

Nark, Lt. Col. Janis 181
Nash, Graham 79
Niebuhr, Gustav 8
Nivola, Costantino 20

O

Obenchain, Rev. John C. 185

P

Pace, Gen. Peter 141
Papas, Pete 185
Papas, Tamora 185
Parker, O'Donald 185
Payne, Mariah 6, 183
Percoco, Jim 149, 172
Perno, Jessica 183
Perot, H. Ross 17, 25
Perot, H. Ross Jr. 147
Peters, Benjamin 185
Petress, Ken 147, 152
Petros, Bill 6
Poling, Barclay 6
Pontes, Colleen 113
Porter, Ginni 185
Powell, Gen. Colin 8, 78, 79, 93, 95, 202
Price, Brig. Gen. George 27, 36, 117, 198, 202
Price, Leontyne 78
Prince, Donna 6, 112, 185
Pruett, Ann 112
Pulliam, Betty 202

R

Radez, Dick 14
Reagan, Nancy 7, 17, 29, 30
Reagan, President Ronald 7, 29, 30, 31, 79
Richardson, Frank 185
Rihn, Kelly Coleman 95, 113, 185

Robb, Charles 93
Robinson, Harry 168, 179, 181
Rockefeller, Sen. Jay 202
Roosevelt, President Franklin Delano 14, 147, 148 *(photo)*
Rosati, James 20
Rosenblatt, Roger 147
Rotondi, Holly 6, 91, 111, 117, 124, 125, 183
Roussey, Sgt. Christopher 81
Rozek, Paul J. 185
Rumley Family 6
Rumley, Beatrice 61
Rumley, Mark 3, 58, 59 *(photo)*, 60 *(photo)*, 61
Rumley, Martha 61
Rumley, Michael 60 *(photo)*, 61
Rumley, Robert 61
Rumley, Robert Patrick, Jr. 3, 58, 61
Rumley, Stephen 60 *(photo)*, 61

S

Sasaki, Hideo 20
Scavone, Dave 6
Schaet, Col. Don 17
Scruggs, Becky 11, 13, 25, 33
Scruggs, Jan 6, 8, 10 *(photo)*, 11, 13, 14, 15, 16, 17, 20, 23, 25, 26 *(photo)*, 27, 29, 30, 33, 45, 57, 58, 59 *(photo)*, 71, 78, 91, 92, 93, 117, 125, 131, 156, 157, 159, 172, 175, 177, 179, 181, 183
Scruggs, Philip K. 185
Searcy, Chuck 91, 183
Segal, Mark 6
Shugarts, William 6
Sidey, Hugh 27
Sigona, Suzanne 111, 185
Simmons, Jerold 157
Smith, Barbara 183
Smith, Cindy 185
Smith, Edward 147
Smith, Walter 6
Smoyer, Nancy 100, 110, 120, 121, 185
Sood, Rajni 6
Spiher, Bruce 15
Spreiregen, Paul 19, 20, 21, 23, 24, 25
Stancliff, Cyndy 113, 185
Stancliff, Paul 113, 185
Staniski, S.J. 6
Stepanek, Jim 185
Stepanek, Marcia 185
Stockdale, Adm. James J. 17
Struck, Doug 147
Struck, William 185
Stufflebean, Ron 185
Sturken, Marita 152, 177
Swerdlow, Joel 27

T

Tabor, Tom 185, 194
Taft, Chuck 73

INDEX

Talley, Regina 185
Taylor, Elizabeth 16
Thacker, Brian 76
Times, Edward L. 176 *(photo)*, 177

V

Versace, Roque 136 *(photo)*, 137

W

Wahlquist, Andy 27
Wallace, Alan 185
Waller, JoAnn 183
Walters, Larry R. 185
Warner, Sen. John 16, 17, 25, 26

(photo), 27, 36, 172, 176 *(photo)*, 177, 202
Watkins, Glenn E. 185
Watt, James 27
Webb, James 17, 25, 29
Weese, Harry 20, 21, 24
Weinberger, Caspar 30
Wenner, Kelly 185
West, Pam 131, 137, 140, 160, 168
Westmoreland, Gen. William 13, 17, 33
Wheeler, Jack 14, 15, 16, 17, 19, 20, 29, 30, 33, 36, 135

Whitebird, Frances 95
Wiesenfeld, Paddy 110, 185
Wiles, Geoff 183
Wilke, Walter 196
Wolcott, Ann 202
Wood, Marilyn 51
Woods, John O. 14, 20, 23, 24, 33, 181
Worstell, Ron 117, 185

Z

Zengerle, Joseph 20